Letters from
EVEREST

OC Rowe
British Everest Exp.
c/. British Ambassador
Katmandu

BRITISH MOUNT EVEREST
EXPEDITION. 1953

CAMP BASE

BY AIR MAIL
PAR AVION

Miss E. J. Lowe,
'Sunny bank',
Hastings,
New Zealand.

GEORGE LOWE

Letters from
EVEREST

Edited and Introduced by
HUW LEWIS-JONES

Foreword by JAN MORRIS
Afterword by PETER HILLARY

SILVERBEAR
an imprint of Polarworld

The stone grows old.
Eternity is not for stones.
But I shall go down from this airy space,
    this swift white peace, this stinging exultation.
And time will close about me, and my soul
    stir to the rhythm of the daily round.
Yet, having known, life will not press so close,
    and always I shall feel time ravel thin about me;
For once I stood
In the white windy presence of eternity.
        Eunice Tietjens, 1917

All men dream: but not equally. Those who dream by night in the dusty recesses of their minds wake in the day to find that it was vanity; but the dreamers of the day are dangerous men, for they may act their dream with open eyes, to make it possible.
        Thomas Edward Lawrence, 1922

First published in the United Kingdom in 2013 by Silverbear, an imprint of Polarworld.

Letters from Everest © Polarworld

The right of Huw Lewis-Jones to be identified as the editor of this work has been asserted by him in accordance with the Copyright, Designs and Patents Act 1988.

Photographs © George Lowe Collection. Every effort has been made to seek permission to reproduce those images for which George Lowe does not hold the copyright. We are grateful to individuals who have assisted in this. Any omissions are entirely unintentional and corrections should be addressed to the publisher.

A CIP catalogue record of this book is available from the British Library.

Published in association with the Lowe family, with the support of Stuart Leggatt and Cameron Treleaven.

Direction by Huw Lewis-Jones
Typeset in Sabon by Liz House
Cover concept by Andrew Wightman

ISBN 978-0-9555255-3-7

Printed and bound in Italy by Graphicom, an FSC certified company.

Silverbear is the new imprint of indie publisher Polarworld – a new home for classic accounts and the very best first-hand narratives of exploration and adventure. Discover more about our titles at www.polarworld.co.uk.

CONTENTS

Base Camp.
2nd June

Dear Betty, Mum, Dad & all.

This will be about
so the mail-runner is off to-morrow with all the
important despatches & cables.

Probably at this hour or half day you will hear
by radio of our success:— Ed & Tenzing reached
the summit at 11.30 last Friday 29th May. I was
watching them from S. Col & Great up to meet them
on their descent to camp. It was quite a Emotive

moment. N.Z. was well to the front - as well as the Lhotse face work. I got onto S. Col where, I spent 4 nights & I's days & carried a 50 lb load to Camp IV at 27,900 ft.

I hope to tell you in detail of the last ten days as we march out to Kathmandu.

We reached Base on 31st May & arrived absolutely played out & to-day = after two days of sleeping & eating = we are just hanky up. To-day is a great day we are all around the wireless listening to the coronation service. The snow is just being placed & there is quite a hush amongst the boys.

FOREWORD

Jan Morris

In two senses these memorable letters come, as they say, from the heart. They come from the true heart of a twenty-nine-year-old New Zealander, writing from distant parts to the ones he loved at home. And they come from the conceptual heart of a famous adventure.

In a way those hearts were shared, anyway. George Lowe was a mountaineer of classic stature, straight as they come, indefatigable, unselfish, fine at the long haul and the apparently insoluble obstacle. The adventure was the British Everest Expedition of 1953, the very first to reach the top of the world, and its style, like his, was traditionally dogged, decent and sensible.

Many thousands of words have been written about that expedition in the sixty years since then, but nobody has recalled the emotions of the experience so intimately as George does in these always vivid, often touching letters from Everest. They were written on the spot, at the moment, and sent to his sister Betty in New Zealand for distribution among their family. He writes about matters petty and monumental, comical and disturbing, frivolous and fateful, about oxygen rates and tinned peas and friendships and perilous crevasses, all with the same frankness and homely clarity. So he elevates a terrific experience to the level of ordinary human understanding.

The world was to grow familiar with the names of Edmund Hillary and Tenzing Norgay, the two who reached the top of the mountain, and of John Hunt the leader who got them there. Lowe was to remain more private, but he was essential to the character and success of the venture. There was no phase of the expedition in which he did not play a vital part, spending long periods at extreme heights, ready to turn his hand at any task, step in at any emergency and tackle the most demanding stages of the route. Hillary, his life-long friend, said afterwards that if Lowe had been in the summit party he would certainly have got to the top, and anyone who reads these letters will have no doubt about it, either. No sense of disappointment or irony weakens them. George enjoyed himself on Everest, and what he told his Betty was all honest, all happy, and all true.

His attitudes exactly mirrored those of the expedition itself, which remains as admirable an exploit as it seemed in 1953. A few petty disputes tarnished its reputation for a time – who got to the top first? – why wasn't Tenzing knighted like Hillary? – and several thousand men and women have climbed Everest since. To my mind, though, there was something essentially decent about John Hunt's expedition, something almost innocent to its triumph, that has made its memory affectionately cherished to this day.

History has helped. Halfway through the twentieth century the British nation was approaching the end of its career as a great world power – signing off, though its people did not always recognize it, after so many victories, such grand tragedies and accomplishments. As it happened in that very year a new young Queen of England was about to succeed to the throne, and visionaries hoped that her accession might mark a sort of rebirth, the start of a new Elizabethan age.

On 2 June 1953, Elizabeth II was crowned at Westminster, and on that very morning the news broke in London that Everest had been climbed. Not only the nation, but people around the world rejoiced at the conjunction. For the Empire, however, it was not a revival but a final hurrah. Yet the Everest success endures far beyond this. These letters from the mountain bear witness to the character of a historic event – and to the character of a good man, too.

* * *

INTRODUCTION

Huw Lewis-Jones

The first ascent of Everest in the summer of 1953 was one of the twentieth century's great triumphs of exploration. Its symbolism as a human achievement, perhaps more so than its usefulness, means that it will always be remembered fondly, often proudly, by those who were alive when word of the success spread across the world. For the generations that follow, and for those of us who discover the story anew for ourselves, it is something, perhaps, of a different age. It shares in the heroism and adventure of history's explorers, yet stands at that precious moment before our race launched itself wildly into space in a blaze of rockets and radar screens. In that, it seems to me at least to sum up the best of the human spirit, in enterprise, daring, and downright hard work. These were the qualities that would lead to that sublime moment when man set foot at last upon the highest point on Earth.

George Lowe was one of two New Zealanders on the Everest expedition, and his efforts on the mountain were crucial to the endeavour. He was one of the lead climbers, forging the route up Everest's Lhotse Face without oxygen and later cutting steps

New Zealander George Lowe on the South Col of Everest in 1953.

for his partners up the summit ridge. He 'put up a performance', described the expedition leader John Hunt, 'which will go down in the annals of mountaineering as an epic achievement of tenacity and skill'. For his own part, George was just happy to be on the mountain sharing in the teamwork of something incredible; doing something he loved. Chosen by his dear friend and climbing partner Ed Hillary to be his 'best man' when married after the Everest success, Lowe was a modest fellow who never sought the limelight. Almost ninety years old now, his achievements deserve wider recognition.

As a historian, it's not often that you have the chance to meet your heroes and, better still, to be given the honour of working with them. Though George's health has now declined, he is still with us and that is something to treasure. Of the Everest climbers of 1953 only George remains.

Over the course of creating George's Everest memoirs, just recently published, and gathering together materials from his rich lifetime of adventure, I came across a small bundle of letters at his house neatly tucked away at the bottom of an oak chest. Sometime later, another small cluster of dusty envelopes appeared, their distinctive red and blue edges calling out, buried within a large stack of faded newspapers. Then, whilst slowly sorting through some old glass slides, a handful more were revealed. George's wife Mary was delighted and after a bit more rummaging pulled a file down from a high shelf. Inside were yet more letters, including many that George had gathered when returning home to New Zealand after the Everest celebrations had quietened down. In time other members of his family also shared their memories and gradually this collection of correspondence has come together.

Though more letters will surely find their way home, we now have a complete narrative of his days on Everest. In this special book a trove of these unpublished letters are brought together for the first time to describe the day-by-day moments of this historic expedition as never before. They provide us with a rare glimpse of private hopes and very public achievements.

These letters are offered here in full in the manner that George hoped for them to be shared with his loved ones, perhaps to be published someday, before his eventful life took him all over the world and consigned the letters to safekeeping. Time passed and attentions, as always, moved elsewhere. Though some minor edits have been made for clarity, original spelling and punctuation, and other idiosyncrasies, have been retained. During his travels George wrote letters home to his family as often as he could. In turn, they could then keep their friends updated with news, frequently before the local newspapers had full accounts of his climbs. Yet these letters were more than just news – George also wrote in case he and his friend Ed never returned to tell the tale.

* * *

George Lowe was born in 1924 in Hastings, a small town on New Zealand's North Island, the seventh child of Archibald and Teenie. His father was a fruit farmer known locally for his fine nectarines and pears, some twenty-seven varieties of apples, and his equally prodigious clan of active children. George's eldest sister Betty, ten years his senior, helped take care of the family throughout her life and they were all very close. After George, came a younger brother, bringing the tally of Lowe children to eight. The majority of the letters George wrote from Everest were to his long-suffering sister Betty, who then had the mammoth task of making multiple hand-written copies to share with the family.

Providing a growing circle of admirers with regular correspondence was a daunting prospect for carefree George. At sea, shortly after leaving Australia, he hatched a plan to cope with replying to a pile of letters, all wishing him luck on the expedition. 'I have an idea that means work for you,' he wrote to Betty in February 1953, 'but it will probably be a good thing.' He went on to explain his plan. He'd write one letter to Betty at every chance he had to jot his thoughts down and she would then share them at home with their folks and the brothers and sisters.

Betty had the task of copying each letter twice by hand, lest an original go astray, and then getting some more typed up by a local lady. Extracts could then be read out, with considerable pride, at George's tramping club. Betty also had a list (it grew to about twenty addresses) to which she would send on some copies. The names included George's old climbing friends, and a few old girlfriends too, whilst the rest could be sent where Betty liked as long as the postage wasn't 'too awful'. 'This will save me a tremendous amount of repetition and it will enable me to give you longer and more detailed news,' he explained by way of an apology, before adding, 'but please be careful that the copies don't get to the press!'

During the march out from Kathmandu George wrote copiously, relaxing by streams in the morning sunshine or scribbling by hurricane lamp then torch-light into the night, too excited to sleep. As they climbed ever higher on the mountain writing became more difficult but he stuck to his task. From

Camp III on 8 May: 'I've just had to have the ink bottle thawed over the primus to fill my pen – I had it in my boot thinking it may have escaped the cold – temperatures at night here are recorded at -30°F'. Halfway up the Lhotse Face and running out of ink, he radioed down to the lower camps and soon one of his companions lent him a much-coveted biro pen (in return for some extra tins of tomato juice). The biro was at its best when warmed gently inside his sleeping bag and in the tough conditions of the climb it worked a treat.

Events moved so swiftly it was often hard to find a moment to write but George would make up for missed days by producing energetic accounts when he had a spare hour or two. Safely in his tent, he wrote until he was too tired to hold a pen and then took refuge in well-earned sleep. Back safely at Base Camp, and reunited with his supply of ink, he was able to fill in all the details at length. And thank goodness he did so. These rare letters from Everest now allow us to travel back in time to join his companions every step of the way: a vivid, behind-the-scenes witness of a climb that would make history. In clear and elegant prose, this is a unique testimony of a superlative human achievement.

* * *

George has been called the 'forgotten man' of Everest, an unsung hero of sorts. Some say his achievements have been overlooked as eyes are drawn to the triumph of the summit or to the disasters and controversy on the mountain of more recent years. George is passed by, perhaps, because he played his part so well. He was a master of his craft, on ice and snow, and a central figure in ensuring the success of the final pair – Ed and Tenzing – who would step up onto the summit that day in May.

Lowe first met Hillary while working in New Zealand's Southern Alps just after the war and they soon struck up a friendship. Little did they know it would be the beginning of a journey to the highest altitudes and latitudes on the planet. Ed would later write that it was George who 'set off the spark that finally got us both to the Himalayas'. In 1951 the pair joined the first New Zealand expedition there, exploring the Indian Garhwal and being part of the team that climbed the 23,760 ft Mukut Parbat.

The following year, thanks to Ed, George was invited by Eric Shipton to join the British expedition to climb Cho Oyu (26,865 ft), the formidable next-door neighbour to Everest and the sixth highest peak in the world. They found a possible way up from the northwest side of Cho Oyu, but with a severely stretched supply chain Ed and George only reached 22,500 ft before they were turned back by dangerous ice-cliffs. Shipton suggested that they might like to have a go at crossing for the first time a pass to the east of Cho Oyu called the Nup La. The young pair agreed without hesitation.

In June 1952 they crossed the Himalayan divide from Nepal down onto the immense glaciers of Tibet to secretly explore the north side of Everest. It took them six days to cover just four miles. The experience remains, in George's estimation, the most exacting and satisfying mountaineering that they had ever undertaken. Standing on the Rongbuk Glacier, Ed wrote: 'There was Everest, proud and aloof against a wind-streaked sky. The glacier was a shining pathway of ice sweeping up to the foot of the mountain.' They managed to explore over halfway

George and Ed Hillary at the Malte Brun Hut, near the upper Tasman Glacier in 1951. They became good friends climbing in New Zealand before heading to the Himalayas together.

round the great northern flank ridges of Everest and eventually clambered back into Nepal, though they had for some time to keep their journey a secret.

Within days George and Ed set off on their next adventure with Shipton and Charles Evans, with just what they stood up in, plus only a sleeping bag, lilo, down jacket and a few exposures left in their cameras. In fact, George recalls, he had less than he would have had for a weekend tramp in New Zealand. Their aim was to get onto the Barun Glacier – an unexplored ice stream between Everest and Makalu (27,838 ft), the fifth highest in the world. Makalu had never been approached before and reaching the head of the Barun and looking into Tibet from there would complete a circuit of Everest over its highest passes.

After exploring many virgin valleys the team eventually retreated, wading knee-deep in new snow, falling in up to the shoulders in masked crevasses and generally having a bleak time. With the monsoon upon them, they got out and down to grass level and then 'hitched their belts' very seriously this time, because 'we were going to try to follow the Barun Glacier and river to its junction with the Arun River, almost twenty miles away, through gorges galore and formidable jungle', George recalls. But this sort of thing was 'bread and meat' to Shipton who thought that this way of finishing a trip, by 'exploring to the very end, was the choicest delight'.

The following year, as is now well known, George was an integral part of the successful Everest expedition, leading the route up the Lhotse Face towards the South Col. Together with Alf Gregory and Sherpa Ang Nima, he supported Ed and Tenzing by placing a final advance camp just 300 m below the summit. More expeditions followed: to Makalu in 1954, again with Ed Hillary, although the mountain was not climbed. Then, after meeting Vivian Fuchs, he and Ed were invited to join the Commonwealth Trans-Antarctic Expedition. George, ever versatile, was given the job of filming the first crossing of the continent. His still imagery and footage are a lasting tribute to his skills and his courage as an explorer with a bewildering array of talents. 'He was,' Ed Hillary described, 'just such a good fellow. Gentle, brilliant, and humble. Simply first-class.' High praise indeed, from this most respected of mountain men.

As we can read in these letters, it was George who first embraced Ed and Tenzing as they made their way down from the summit of Everest, that brilliant May day back in 1953. George had been observing their progress from high on the Col and climbed up to meet them as they descended. He brought with him a thermos of warm tomato soup. Ed unclipped his mask, grinned a tired greeting and then sat down on the ice for a rest. Finally looking up to his old friend, he said in his matter-of-fact way: 'Well, George, we knocked the bastard off!'

* * *

Mount Everest, the highest mountain in the world, attracts attention like no other. From its southern approaches it dominates the Khumbu region of Nepal, far to the northeast of Kathmandu. Triangulated as Peak XV in 1856, the mountain was named soon after in honour of Sir George Everest, a former Surveyor General of India, though of course the mountain had been known about for centuries. To the Nepalese she is Sagarmatha, to the Tibetans

Chomolungma – Goddess Mother of the Earth – the jewel of the Himalaya, a range that stretches for over 1,500 miles from Kashmir to Assam. It is generally agreed that the main summit is a formidable 29,029 ft (8,848 m), and the mountain is actually slowly growing taller each year – some 5 mm, scientists suggest – uplifted as the Indian tectonic plate pushes northwards into Asia.

First seen by a non-native in 1849, the earliest attempt to climb Everest followed over seventy years later. The successful 1953 expedition was the ninth attempt on the mountain, leaving aside three solo endeavours and an abortive, unofficial Russian venture. Up to the end of 2011, at a reasonable reckoning, there had been 5,640 successful ascents by 3,450 individual climbers. At the beginning of 1953 there had been none.

Though we now rightly celebrate sixty years of endeavour since the first ascent by Hillary and Tenzing on 29 May 1953, this year is an extraordinary anniversary year in the story of Everest. It is fifty years since an American expedition made the epic first ascent of the West Ridge and also completed the first traverse of the mountain; twenty-five years since the first ascent of a route up the South Buttress on the eastern Kangshung Face; and thirty-five years since the first ascent without supplemental oxygen.

Climbers from around the world still lift their eyes to this summit. If approached respectfully Everest will always offer even the most able of climbers a challenge fit for this queen of the mountains – and she remains an unpredictable, frequently deadly, adversary. Though some 223 people have now died in pursuit of its highest places, and the mountain itself is increasingly commercialised, the hunger for Everest seems to show no sign of abating.

Yet, the mystery of possibility has gone now. As the finest alpinists have set their sights on new technical challenges in other far-flung ranges, Everest refuses to disappear. And why should it? It draws climbers like no other mountain. It stands apart from all others, a challenge to human curiosity, courage, and – dare we say it – to a little of the manageable madness that inhabits all true adventure. It takes a certain type of man, or woman, to want to climb there. The question is not so much *can* Everest be climbed now, but rather can *you* do it too? In old age, and no doubt frustrated at the same old questions, Ed Hillary responded gruffly when asked about Everest as an anniversary of his ascent approached: 'It's all bullshit on Everest these days.' He could be forgiven his frustration. His heroes, as mine, have long since left the mountain.

Back in 1953, climbing Everest was something that was truly newsworthy. Without satellites, the Internet and other modern tools of communication, the expedition was to some extent left to its own devices to get on with the job. And yet, as we learn in George's letters, fierce competition amongst hacks to scoop the latest news reached frenzied heights. *The Times* was so concerned to protect its copyright on dispatches from the expedition, as the major sponsor, it even sent its own Special Correspondent to the mountain to ensure fair play and first news.

And when required, news really could travel fast. Once word of the summit success reached Advance Base Camp on 30 May, as the weary climbers returned, journalist James Morris hurtled down through the Icefall without delay. Early the following morning, he handed a brief message to a waiting runner who carried it almost twenty miles to a little radio outpost in the nearest village. The Indian Vice-Consul forwarded the coded message to the British Ambassador in Kathmandu who then sent a confidential cipher to England, transmitting the news some 4,500 miles and five hours back in time to the Foreign Office in London. The Office informed *The Times*, where the news was received in Fleet Street at around tea-time on 1 June. The Queen was given word on the eve of her Coronation and it was in all the newspapers the next day.

It was a triumph for humankind and yet the timing was such that it was a very British achievement. 'The ascent of Everest by a British expedition is a new, timely and brilliant jewel in the Queen's diadem', ran one English newspaper. 'It called for a combination of mountaineering skill, resolution, scientific study and logistic planning, such as no comparable enterprise has received. The credit of the two climbers who actually reached the summit – Hillary and Tenzing – is only in the final stage a personal one. It is much more the flowering of a collective effort in which all have shared, not forgetting the members of previous expeditions, for each team that goes to Everest stands on the shoulders of the one before it.'

A true sentiment, yet that same newspaper, *The Guardian*, also concluded that the mountain 'is in its nature a terminal point; it is like one of those great peaks that stand a little aside from the main chain of the range. It is doubtful whether anyone will ever try to climb Everest again now that it has been done'. How wrong they were. The ascent of Mont Blanc in 1786 didn't put an end to interest in Alpine mountaineering, after all, and Everest was the biggest of all the Himalaya. Their success sparked a brief golden age of mountaineering. Of the fourteen mountains above 8,000 m only Annapurna had been scaled when Hillary and Tenzing stood on top of Everest. Just five weeks later, the world's ninth highest peak, Nanga Parbat, was topped and by the end of that decade only Shishapangma, which lay off-limits in Chinese occupied Tibet, remained unconquered.

When so many Himalayan climbs in the intervening years have been attempted out of national jingoism, commercial opportunism, or personal egotism and misadventure, there is still something reassuring in the thought that most of the men who went to Everest became climbers simply for the joy that the mountains bring, and were drawn there in 1953 purely for the physical and mental challenge of this remarkable place. In working together on his mountain memoirs, *The Conquest of Everest*, George offered this elegant summary:

For me, Everest was never really about the superlatives, conquering a mountain, or about an idea of man battling with nature to win some gallant and great fight. I let others use that language back in 1953, and they were free to do so. For me, it was simply about wanting to be there. The deep desire that I had to go and try – making the most of the opportunity to be part of something significant and to give my very best. I could do nothing more.

George recalls Ed Hillary's well-known comment, 'It is not the mountain we conquer but ourselves.' All the men who went there were much changed by the Everest experience and that is why it was such a special time in their lives. As George explained recently:

From the top of the Khumbu Icefall, where George took this shot, mighty Everest towers over everything.

When Ed Hillary took this photograph on 29 May just four men had seen this final ridge to the summit of Everest – and none had set foot there.

We were a group of people that had gathered together from all corners of the world, yet we nonetheless quickly became a team of friends – it was an expedition that has become a life-long meeting of friends. It has rewarded me in ways that are impossible to sum up. I will forever be grateful for Everest and for my other journeys in the Himalaya. To me the mountains are not a place for competition. The mountains are just where you want to be. Before we arrived Everest was still a dream. It was available for doubt and uncertainty. It still remained that way after we left. As Wilf Noyce so beautifully wrote, 'Men we descend, Conquerors never'. Within days the drifting snows had covered our footprints.

So, let us now join George – as the young New Zealander, just twenty-nine years old – at the beginning of a great adventure that would shape the rest of his life. He has arrived in India and the work of the 1953 Everest expedition is just beginning. What follows are his remarkable words, written with delight as these historic events unfold. This is his story.

* * *

Members of the 1953 Everest expedition on the first day of the approach march. Back row, from left to right: Stobart, Pugh, Noyce and Evans. Middle row: Band, Ward, Hillary, Bourdillon and Westmacott. Front row: Gregory, Lowe, Hunt, Tenzing and Wylie.

THE 1953 BRITISH
MOUNT EVEREST EXPEDITION

John Hunt (1910-1998), aged 42 on Everest, *expedition leader*

Charles Evans (1918-1995), 33, *deputy leader, climbing party*

Charles Wylie (1921-2007), 32, *organising secretary, climbing party*

Tenzing Norgay (1914-1986), 39, *sirdar, climbing party*

Edmund Hillary (1919-2008), 33, *climbing party*

George Lowe (1924-), 29, *climbing party*

Wilfrid Noyce (1917-1962), 35, *climbing party*

George Band (1929-2011), 24, *climbing party*

Alfred Gregory (1913-2010), 39, *climbing party*

Tom Bourdillon (1924-1956), 28, *climbing party*

Michael Westmacott (1925-2012), 28, *climbing party*

Michael Ward (1925-2005), 27, *doctor*

Griffith Pugh (1909-1994), 43, *physiologist*

Tom Stobart (1914-1980), 38, *cameraman*

James Morris (1926-), 26, The Times *correspondent*

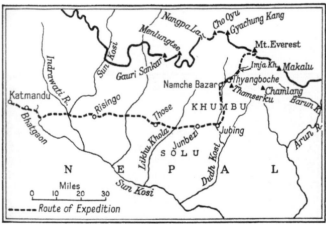

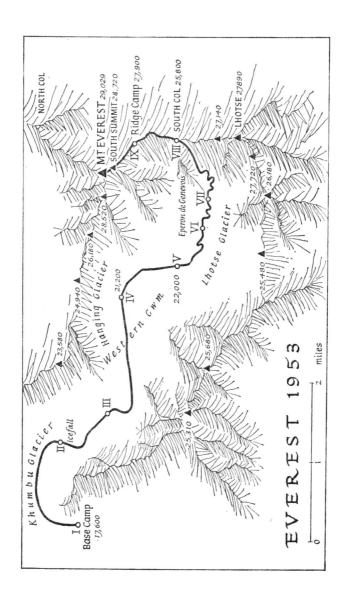

EVEREST 1953

NORTH COL

MT. EVEREST 29,029
SOUTH SUMMIT 28,720
Ridge Camp 27,900
SOUTH COL 25,800
LHOTSE 27890

IX
VIII
27,140
28,520
26,180
26,180
Eperon de Genevois
VI VII
27,720
24,940
21,200
Hanging Glacier
23,580
IV
22,000
Western Cwm
Lhotse Glacier
25,480
25,680
V
III
Icefall
25,310
II
Khumbu Glacier
I
Base Camp
17,600

0   1   2
miles

Letters from

EVEREST

CHAPTER ONE

Taj Mahal Hotel, Bombay
20th February 1953

Dear Betty,

Yesterday morning I stepped ashore at Bombay and work began. A local business man met me and with his car and efficiency I saw to several matters. Bombay is not too hot at present and the day was very pleasant. Today his car is calling at 11 a.m. and then I'll be off on the rounds of people and offices.

The Taj Mahal Hotel is the largest and best known in Bombay – a huge place with a thousand servants and great gardens. I have 'a room' at 35 rupees per day (with all meals – 35 rupees = £3 approximately), which consists of lavatory, shower, bathroom, writing room with two lounge chairs and a fan, a bedroom with twin beds, built-in lighting, an electric clock, another fan, and a marble inlaid floor! (charged to the Expedition.)

I'm fit and well – I shall be glad when these 8 days are ended. The work is tedious and Bombay is quite a lonely place. I'm looking forward to seeing the other boys.

I hope all is well at home. Love to all the family.

More anon, George.

British Everest Expedition
c/o U.K. High Commissioner, New Delhi
24th February 1953

Dear Betty,

Phew it's hot! – at least it was, but I have my tie off and am writing this in an air-conditioned Bombay office. The Himalayan Club Secretary is a big business man here and he has looked after me with free use of his home, car and chauffeur, his clubs and meals, his office and its facilities and his knowledge of the influential people of Bombay; and, too, I have been included in tennis parties and dinner parties. All in all he has been a heaven-sent aid in a hell-hole of heat and government red tape.

I am fit and well, eating ravenously and despite heat and office work I'm becoming fatter – if not fitter. There have been many more things to attend to now that I have been in Bombay for a few days and the most tedious are the cancellations of air bookings and rebooking fresh ones, adding 20 gallons of kerosene to the lot which has already gone forward – there are no suitable jerry cans in Bombay. The packing of the wireless gear, walkie-talkie sets and receiver sets is quite fun – all have to be tested.

The customs officers have to be seen regularly and we are arguing about the expedition food. They claim that we should pay customs duty on that food which is consumed in India. We argue that the food will be consumed in Nepal, a separate country, and they cannot charge us customs on that. It will take a day or two to clear this up. The railways will not so far attach a special waggon carrying out 8 tons of equipment onto the fast express by which we intend travelling from Bombay. We think the chance of theft and pilfering is too high to risk having it sent by goods train. This argument will take a few days and may not be settled completely to our advantage.

Tomorrow I am going to Poona by the 'Deccan Queen' (an express train) to stay for a day with Professor Finch, the director of National Chemical Laboratories, to discuss oxygen and also to see a Dr. Roy about the formalities to be observed in receiving broadcasts of meteorological reports over the All India radio. These are special bulletins for the Everest party and trace the arrival and speed of onset for the year's monsoon. On Friday 27th I will be motoring back to Bombay with Prof. Finch who would like to meet the Everest Party, who arrive on the 'Stratheden' on the 28th Feb. The local big-shots of Bombay have organised a big reception party for the Everest team and the officers of the H.M.S. Ceylon – a cruiser which has just arrived here with a rear-admiral aboard – and this party is to take place at a fashionable home in Bombay hills next Saturday night. Bags of whisky and soda, pot-bellies, bon homies and walrus moustaches – you can imagine the picnic. "Hello old man, I met you in Poona in '38, ah jolly good show, what!" and speeches and toasts. I'm looking forward to it and will report in detail if I get time.

Last weekend I went to A.H. Leyden's home at the fashionable residential quarter called Pali Hill, 12 miles from the centre of the city. I have been staying there ever since in luxury and good fellowship. He is German born but has a British nationalized Swiss wife. They have a beautiful garden, an equally beautiful home and a passion for great big greyhounds which live in the house and are fussed over, preened over and fed like fighting cocks. Leyden is a talented artist and his oil paintings of the mountains and villages in the Himalaya are the most striking and attractive that I have ever seen. Usually oils are dull paintings but his are full of sunshine and dramatic lighting effects that I find quite exciting.

Last Saturday I played tennis at Pali Hill and then dressed in my best bib and tucker (dinner suit) and after a lavish buffet dinner we moved next door to a dance which was held on the terraced lawns of the neighbour's garden, chairs and tables and whisky provided. The place was flood-lit and a good gramaphone and amplifier supplied the noise for dancing. A powdered tarpaulin was used to dance on and with the moon and stars, the flowers in bloom and the gushing talk of the overdressed wives it was like the films. Sunday I swam at the Juhu beach and played more tennis. Monday and today back to office duties.

News hasn't run out, the paper has.

Love, George.

British Everest Expedition
c/o U.K. High Commissioner, New Delhi
27th February 1953

Dear Folks,

I am having a very memorable time in India – in fact a more wonderful and eventful trip than I have ever had previously. I didn't think that I would enjoy the time in Bombay so much. Actually I am now in Poona in Professor G.I. Finch's spacious fan-cooled office. The temperature is 99°F. today, calm and clear with air like a furnace outside. My lips and face are dry and a bit sore from the change to such dry evaporating heat.

Yesterday afternoon I came up to Poona, 2,000 ft and 150 miles inland on a table-land with the jagged teeth of the Western Ghats – a range of hills – showing along the horizon. At 5.10 p.m. I stepped aboad the 'Deccan Queen', a fast electric train to Poona and we streaked out of Bombay, whistling and whizzing through the suburban stations at quite exciting speeds. The sun sets early here at present and we slammed across the coastal plain as the sun went down behind the hills. It was hot, searing hot, the wind was like a flame-thrower through the window. I think that's how my lips and skin became so dry and sore. With only two stops and a steep climb up the Western Ghats – travelling still at a high rate – we skidded to a halt in Poona after 2½ hours.

The Professor and his wife met me at the station and whisked me off in the Zephyr Six to a dinner with two doctors and two brigadiers. Professor Finch is the director of National Chemical Laboratories – a huge central building with a whole colony of houses round about. Fundamental scientific experiment is their chosen task and I saw over the place today. There are researches into x-ray; x-ray of crystals to compare their atomic structure; artificial manufacture of blood plasma from sheep's bones and gelatine; artificial manufacture of sapphires that are perfect crystals to be used as jewel bearings in intricate machinery, the culture of enzymes and bacteria for the growth of plants and the breaking down of coffee, and a thousand other possible purposes; another bloke is attempting to find a bacteria that will act on a compound to precipitate pure sulphur.

... Bombay. Friday 27th.

Life moves rapidly. I talked all afternoon with Finch mostly about oxygen and discussed with him the physiology of high altitude – he is lecturing to some people this evening with slides. I am going along and then joining him for dinner. In Poona for 2 hours we met the director of meteorology for India and discussed and fixed with his department an arrangement to have the weather forecast broadcast to us over All India radio and the BBC (short wave) at 13.50 hours GMT. This will be a special service for us during May and the first week of June. They are to give the wind velocities in the altitudes of 25,000 to 30,000 feet and the warning of the approach of the real monsoon and the westerly disturbances (the "little monsoon") which occur before the main onset. We intend to climb on during the westerly disturbances but retreat smartly when the real monsoon begins. They guarantee to give us four days notice.

The Secretary of the English Alpine Club arrived in Poona – Basil Goodfellow is his name, and the name is very appropriate – and with he and Finch talking I learned a lot. The oxygen equipment this year is of three types. The main standby consists of a 10 lb. cylinder of oxygen with a valve and flow control and a rubber tube going straight into the mouth and held by the teeth. The climber trains himself to breathe in normally while the tube allows a 3 litre per minute (or more) flow into the lungs to augment the rarified air. In breathing out the user bites the tube and conserves the flow. The supply lasts approximately 4 hours at 3 litres per minute and the whole thing is then discarded and a new bottle picked up. As far as possible dumps will be made. This simple type is what Finch thinks is "the goods". His theory is the simpler the better. With augmented breathing apparatus he claims we'll breathe less rapidly and move more quickly. Weight, claustrophobia, irritation due to pure oxygen will be avoided and the chance of breakdown in supply is very slight. He is surprised that this method has not been tried since his experiment in 1922. (He reached 27,300 ft by this method in 1922 – on Everest.)

The other types are a 30 lb. 'closed circuit' type developed by Tom Bourdillon and his father. It consists of a mask and back pressure valves and hopes to conserve the moisture and warmth normally dissipated when breathed out. The set is heavy and complicated – if it works it's the best idea of the three – but if it doesn't you're a dead duck.

The third is an idea of Secords using the chemical called 'something' tetroxide which gives off oxygen when breathed on by carbon dioxide. The Swiss had this and found the oxygen flowed off too quickly and was lost or wasted. So Secord is developing a Heath Robinson idea of a bladder lined waistcoat that collects and inflates with the oxygen given off by the chemical breathed upon. When the chemical is exhausted the container is thrown away and the waistcoat full of air supplies the climber. This is not yet ready and little faith is placed in the system.

... 1st March.

In two hours I'll be aboard the express and heading for Lucknow. The English boys arrived yesterday and although I had met none of them – they were like meeting old friends. Wylie and Ward I took an immediate liking to – the others are quieter. Noyce is reserved, slow of speech and probably the most 'prosaic' and undemonstrative – a master at Charterhouse school – married – 35. Westmacott is just on 28 – a statistician – whatever that is. This is his first Himalayan trip – done a lot of Alpine ascents and looks a good type. George Band is the baby – 6 ft 2 and 24 years old. Still a student at Cambridge (geology) and counted as by far the most outstanding of the youngest generation in Britain. All are super rock climbers with a fair experience of snow-craft. Stobart is 6 ft 3 and 14½ stone – a giant blonde. He's the cameraman – been to the Antarctic and nearly every country in the world – except N.Z. – age 38.

Names will be a problem because there are two Toms; two Michaels; two Georges; and two Charles. This is rather an amazing number of duplications amongst 13 people.

Yesterday everything went smoothly. The baggage (454 pieces) was unloaded and transferred to a special wagon – 8 tons in all. All details of entry were settled and we had a fairly easy day.

Last night was this big party – seventy people at the show – in one of the beautiful and fashionable homes on Pali Hill. The supper was a work of art. The most outstanding creation was two great dishes with whole cooked fish – each about three feet long (the fish) and adorned with the fanciest of colours, with patterns of tomato and cucumber setting them off. Today we spent the morning swimming on Juhu beach and the afternoon chatting over tea in a very cool garden. And now we are off on the tedious rail journey to the border.

I have sent two parcels from Bombay, one contains a book – 'Annapurna' and the other trinkets that I would like you to hold on to – namely 2 coconut shell dishes, 2 small vases, a sandal wood elephant and a book on Victoria, Australia. Enclosed is a cutting from today's paper.

Love to all the folks.

Smiles, George.

British Embassy, Katmandu
9th March 1953

Dear Betty,

Five of us left Bombay by train on 1st March and after five days on the Indian railways we reached Rapaul on the Nepal border and after two more days of truck and walking we reached Katmandu along with the eight tons of baggage that goes with this expedition. The journey was a tedious drag and the shepherding of the baggage made for a lot of worry and delay. It's all here now and while the boys that flew in are receiving and checking the loads we are having a well earned spell.

It's a beautiful day here in Katmandu. Cool and fresh like a spring day at home, birds singing and carefully tended spring flowers blooming in the Embassy garden. This is a wonderful place after the stinking hot Indian plains and the sultry sweating in Bombay.

The train journey across India – from Bomaby to Lucknow – was the usual hot, changeless, half sleeping two days. Two things of note – the first, we stopped at a deserted place on the line and on enquiry found that the engine had blown the cylinder-head off. A relief engine rescued us 3 hours later. The second thing was personal – and much more lasting. I had dysentery for five days and the journey was very miserable. I had violent stomach pains, a feverish temperature and some very uncomfortable moments. I lost 7 pounds in weight and went right off food. Michael Ward (the party doctor) was with me and with his nursing and sulphur drugs I came round O.K. I was feeling rather weak but managed the 24 mile walk into Katmandu yesterday. It is not surprising that I am ravenously hungry now and quite stiff in the muscles after the two months of boat and hotel living. Of all the times and places to suffer this infliction I think I would pick a train journey. If it had happened after the expedition had left I would have been left behind.

But, in Lucknow, I was not so sick that I could not drag to a car and go and see the 'Residency'. This is the historic ruins – a collection of towers, keeps and heavy brick buildings – all roofless and aged with scars and holes made by cannon balls. The Residency is the scene of the famous Seige of Lucknow 1856 or thereabouts. The scene too of "The Pipes of Lucknow" and the doings of the highland regiments during the Indian Mutiny. The place where these unfortunate people (2,000 odd Europeans and faithful Indians) decided to withstand the attack of the mutineers is quite fantastically vulnerable. Yet with straight out blind courage and desperate bravery they defended this spot. About 900 survived after 7 months which must have been hell. After seeing this place and hearing a little of the episode I am really impressed with the effort. The Indian Army keep the place as a great park with masses of bouganvillia and petunias in flower. I took a few colour photographs and expect they'll be good.

We stayed overnight in Lucknow with the local manager of Burmah-Shell – he's a Public School boy of English pattern. He was wonderfully kind and smoothed the way for us – two cars at our disposal and his home. Most of this party are ex Public School types – Marlborough, Shrewsbury, Gordonstoun and Charterhouse – and the old school tie spirit keeps them all together like a Masonic craft. I thought it was very good to see.

The zoo in Lucknow is a good one. It spreads over a huge park area and we drove around looking at lions, rhinos, tigers, hyenas and all number of fowl and birds. The lions were rather wild and most impressive.

Returning to Nepal was not without its pleasure. The sickness was leaving me and I got a certain kick out of crossing the border into this place again. The baggage came in over the mountains on the famous aerial ropeway. This is about 20 miles long and loops across the deep valleys over 2,000 feet above the valley-floor. It must be 1½ miles between the pylons on the longest stretch. Everything seems to have arrived intact so one of the major tasks of the expedition has been accomplished.

Yesterday I got my first view of the snows. We crossed a little pass on the walk in – the valleys are full of green spring growth – and then Michael and I spotted simultaneously the peaks;

incredibly high and blurred by haze away behind. The outline of these Nepal peaks is quite fantastic. There are no rounded mountains here. They jut and sweep up with quite exciting angles – always fluted with ice channels and looking from a distance quite impossible. It is a thrill to look at these hills. If I came 20 times I would still get a kick out of the looking.

Tea is about to be served. I have had a quiet hour – with the Ambassador's radiogram and microgroove records. First a series of carols and now a Beethoven Piano Concerto. All very suitable for a Sunday don't you think. I may add to this later if there is time. Thanks for your letters Betty – I received two (one from Ed) along with 10 others. Lucky aren't I. I hope to reply to thcm all on the march in. Thanks for the numerous cuttings – especially of Enid Westermans daughter and all. Enclosed is an invitation we received to a Bombay party and two photos taken in Poona – plus a French stamp. There's lots more but it will have to wait.

Regards to all the family and everybody, George.

P.S. Tuesday, 10th March. We're off today – in a few minutes in fact. It's been a rare rush but I'm glad to be off. Have had no time for more letters and our personal kit this year is very limited – too limited at present.

More anon.

Love to all, George.

On the March
12th March 1953

Dear Betty and all,

It's dark, the sun sets early here now, about 6.15 p.m. and I'm holding a torch in one hand as it's too early to go to sleep and the kerosene light is too weak to read by. We had completed the third day's march by 1 p.m. today and I have been sun-bathing, sleeping and catching butterflies since then.

Last night we camped on the river bed of the Sun Kosi river. It's winter here and the water is icy cold. The night is perfectly clear. I slept on my eider-down bag as the night was warm. At 5 a.m. we got up and after a mug of tea set out at dawn – 6 a.m. Today we climbed out of the steep Sun Kosi valley up to 7,000 ft and now we are camped high above the valleys and it's only two minutes walk to a great view of the high peaks (we've identified Karyolung, Numbur and Gauri Sankar). On the way up the ridge we had several wonderful views all down the valley. There were flowering peaches and perhaps some flowering almonds and just a few rhododendrons.

In Katmandu we were issued with and fitted with our oxygen masks and urged to wear them on the march in. I put mine on today during the steep uphill and found that when I was hurrying and breathing really hard I forgot that it was on my face and nose. It's an ugly looking thing – a big rubber mask covering the mouth nose and chin. To keep the fitting tight it is necessary to shave, which may cause some bother later with sunburn and even cold.

This evening three of us went for a stroll and looked at the cloud rolling over the range. Later John Hunt and Mike Westmacott came up with butterfly nets and began chasing butterflies. They are collecting specimens for the British Museum. It was fun watching them stalking up to a shrub with a net poised – it seemed incongruous that these hardy mountaineers should be such crack-pot looking butterfly catchers. Later on we joined in the game and found that the hunt was really good fun. We caught some big jet black beauties and some smaller yellow ones. John Hunt seems to know something of the different varieties and has a collection of his own in England.

At sunset the clouds over the peaks rolled away and we ran up to see the peaks turn gold in the setting sun. We ate curried rice, cauliflower, peas, tinned steak and boiled potatoes in the big communal tent and now that it's dark I'm writing this. Most of the boys have taken their lilos and sleeping bags outside and a group of them are identifying stars and planets. George Band seems to be the expert on names and settings – I must knock off or I'll strain my eyes.

... 13th March.

Today is another clear warm day. Ahead of me are the blue ridges and on the skyline are the snow-covered peaks. It's breakfast time and we're sitting on a grassy knoll with ferns and rhododendrons all around. The Sherpas are cooking porridge, bacon and eggs. The butterfly catchers are out again – there are thousands of moths, beetles and butterflies in this forest but the most striking of all are the birds – auriols, shrikes, chats, various finches and of course mynahs and crows. Earlier this morning John Hunt, George Band and I were together and we sat down to listen and watch a bird like a blackbird – perhaps bigger – with two tail feathers at least 15 inches long. It had a bright orange beak and a strident call. As we sat quietly two animals came out of the ferns and crossed the track. They were about 3 feet long with very short legs covered with brown fur. None of us had any idea what they were.

Nearly all of this morning's walk has been over a sort of high rolling moorland covered with grass, thorny bushes, azaleas (not in flower) and dwarf trees. After breakfast the track drops into a deep valley about 2,500 ft downhill and then climbs out of the other side.

It will be another week before this is posted and I hope to keep adding a piece each day or so until the day comes for John Hunt to send his 'Times' despatch.

... 15th March.

Tomorrow John Hunt is going to send a runner with a Times despatch and I'm hurrying before dark to add some more. First, with the help of a book on Indian animals we identified the brown animals as martens – a variety of weasel and stoat only bigger than our home variety. This evening we are camped overlooking the foothills and looking onto the main peaks of the Gauri Sankar range of the Himalaya, about 23,000 ft. The photographers have been busy but now it is very cold and everybody is putting on jerseys and coming into the tent.

By the time you get this I expect we will be up at Thyangboche – our first base camp. We expect to be there on the 27th or 28th March. After two days there we are breaking into sets of 4 men each and going off to climb and practice with our oxygen equipment for eight or ten days and then return to discuss the results and split up and climb with others practicing with oxygen for another 10 days. So I expect it will be some time before you hear reports of us attempting Everest. That won't be until after the middle of May. With this oxygen equipment we have optimistic hopes of success but if we miss in the Spring there will definitely be an Autumn attempt. There are at least four reserves in England organising and waiting for news of this attempt and they will come out and join Hunt plus those of this party who are still fit enough to be of use. Going to high altitudes will exhaust some and they presumably will not be asked to stay, nor is it expected that they will be of use. This is all high conjecture and should not be made too public.

I guess that's all for now. It has been suggested that the expedition address be altered to: c/o British Embassy, Katmandu, Nepal, which I'm sure will be faster and more efficient than New Delhi.

I am looking forward to the next mail delivery which won't be for another two or three weeks. Kindest regards to the people of Heretaunga Tramping Club and all the other interested folks. And to Mum and Dad and all the family. Everyone here is well – Ed is his usual self and until next post,

Cheerio, George.

P.S. Could you let me know to whom you are sending a copy of my letters? I think there were four English addresses and I hope you can share the postage for a copy each, otherwise the letters will never get round fast enough. At present I am planning to go on to England in July and have tentative ideas of a return early next year – say March 1954.

Could you let me know how much my bank account is holding at present? It will be mid-May before you hear any news of us on Everest so by that time you'll be impatient, I expect.

Bye, Geo.

Ed and Tenzing share a joke as they stop for lunch on the trail. Marching in the warm sunshine, many of the team wore shorts and tennis shoes.

CHAPTER TWO

Dudh Kosi Valley
21st March 1953

Dear Betty,

Everest is in view with a huge snow plume blowing away to the East and from here it towers over the Lhotse Nuptse wall (a wall over 25,000 ft high). Now we are walking through the most beautiful part of Nepal. Perhaps I'm biased in favour of alpine scenery but even so the flowers are everywhere, whereas before there were none. There are gushing mountain streams with fern and moss clinging whereas before there were dry gullies.

I've been collecting flowers to really photograph them, but not very successfully. There are the usual blue primulas – whole paddocks of them. I tried to photograph a type of violet that grows in the moss by the waterfalls; and I picked some of these violets, but they died within a few hours. On the hillsides there are plenty of pines and growing amongst these we found a giant daphne, a bush about five or six feet high, entirely without leaves as yet, but with a few blooms that are exactly like our daphne at home, with the scent and all. I wish now that I knew more about botany and could collect and classify some of these flowers. The flowers are far more beautiful this year, mostly because we are a month earlier than last year. This is our twelfth day of the walk in and every day has been hot and windless.

Yesterday we crossed a 12,000 ft pass and although there were patches of snow and pockets of frost in the shade, we crossed in tennis shoes and shorts, and with our shirts off. Every day I've been bare to the sun and am browner than I've ever been in my life. I've never experienced such uniformly perfect weather and it seems more amazing when you consider that 30 miles away Everest is trailing an arctic snow plume.

In five more days we will have reached Thyangboche monastery (13,500 ft), where we intend splitting into 3 groups and going off with oxygen to try the sets up to 20,000 ft and to get acclimatised to altitude before we approach the mountain. The first acclimatisation period will last for 7 days and then we return to Thyangboche and change our parties around and confer on the effects of the oxygen experiments and then off for another ten days practice while one party explores the Khumbu ice-fall and prepares a route for the big weight lift into the Western Cwm. Here, diagrammatically, is what we have been doing since leaving Katmandu – crossing the 'grain' of the country by going over a ridge and down a valley.

Tomorrow the mail is going out, but we won't be getting mail back until about three weeks. I am looking forward to hearing news of home and seeing how you are all getting on.

Love to all, George.

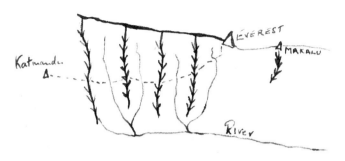

Namche
25th March 1953

Dear Betty,

Today we reached Namche after seventeen days walking. I had often thought before about Namche with its fluted peaks, with a view of Everest at 29,000 ft and down to the Dudh Kosi river that flows through pines at 9,000 ft. I had thought that perhaps my memory of it had glamourised the wonder of it, but it was not so. Today as we walked up the river and through the gorge of the river and then under the overhanging rock walls that hide the Namche track, I decided with Ed and Charles Evans that it was far more impressive than we had ever dreamt. Just after we left the river at only 9,000 ft we got a view of Everest only twelve miles away with the usual snow plume blowing away. It was a terrific size, even though it was twelve miles away, and it was difficult to believe that it was 20,000 ft above us. Oddly enough for this time of year, there is very little snow on the top parts of Everest and we expect some heavy falls in the next few weeks.

Yesterday we had breakfast in the most beautiful place. We stopped at a clearing in heavy forest with frost still on the ground. Nearly every tree around the clearing was either a huge magnolia or rhododendron in full flower. When the sun reached us, the photographers went mad. I took a lot of colour photographs which I hope will show something of the glory of this place. The magnolia blooms were perfectly white and mostly <u>over</u> 12 inches across. These trees are between 40 feet and 60 feet high – covered with blooms and not one leaf. They are difficult to climb, but Ed scaled up one and with a kukri, lopped off a huge limb which enabled us to get some close-up photographs of the separate blooms.

Lately we have collectively seen a lot of animals and birds which we have missed before. Early in the trip we saw a marten (stoat family) and lately a musk deer (very rare), two panthers, a large horned goat like a bharal, several monkeys, and four snakes. The largest snake was crossing the track when Greg and I were together. The track was about 3 ft wide and the head was in the undergrowth on one side while the tail was still slithering through the undergrowth on the other.

I have a feather in my hat which is seventeen inches long and John Hunt (who is a keen bird watcher) tells me that it is the tail feather of a Himalayan tree-pie – a gloriously plumed bird that is quite rarely seen. I found the feather in the bush three days ago.

Tomorrow we walk to Thyangboche (13,500 ft) where we will camp for three days before heading off on the first acclimatisation trip.

More anon from there.

Love to all, George.

Thyangboche Monastery
29th March 1953

Dear Folks,

Thyangboche Monastery is certainly the most beautiful place in all the Himalaya. Everybody here seems to think so. Two years ago Ed wrote to me from here and went into eulogies of praise and Tilman said that he was coming back to die here.

We reached Thyangboche – our present base – two days ago. The day was perfect and we topped the rise at mid-day, to lie in a big grassy paddock set aside for us by the lamas. All around are mountains with the most fantastic shapes and straight ahead of me now is Everest, clear on one side and streaming with a plume of snow and cloud on the other. It looks immensely high and formidable from here (13,000 ft).

... 30th March.

I've been so busy these last two days with food, wireless, oxygen, aluminium bridging, tripod and yacht-tackle bridging, arranging clothing and a dozen other things, that the days have gone like wildfire. Maybe on this trip we're off on today I'll tell you about equipment; of the visit and blessing at the Thyangboche Monastery and of how they pray for us and the Sherpas every day; of how we're having trouble with a pirating newspaper man from the Daily Telegraph (London) who has come to Namche with a wireless and hopes to forestall the 'Times' in 'noos'; of how we listened last night to London direct to the commentary on the Oxford Cambridge boat-race; of how we climbed a peak of 16,000 ft this morning and tested the walky-talky wireless

The team reached Thyangboche Monastery on 27 March and set up camp in a grassy meadow. Later that day they pitched all the tents for the first time, about twenty in all for the various stages up the mountain.

sets (weight 9½ lbs) which worked perfectly; of our various tents which are full of new ideas; of our footgear (down socks, woolly camp-boots, fur-lined general purpose boots, high altitude kapok lined boots, etc.); of a dozen other things.

I've just been out of the tent to see the wonders of sunset on Everest. The rocks were a velvety-black and the snow was pink with a great pink cloud trailing away – it was a great view. Tom Stobart, the photographer, has just been trying to film it.

Well, I must tell you what we're off to do. We're going off in 3 parties to spend 8 days climbing and exploring to get acclimatised and try an oxygen test-run at 18,000 or 20,000 feet. I'm in John Hunt's party along with Gregory and Tenzing and six high-altitude Sherpas (a high altitude Sherpa is one equipped exactly as we are and who we hope will carry to the highest camps on Everest). We are going up the Imja valley under the Lhotse-Nuptse wall to explore a piece of range there for 8 days.

We'll be back in Thyangboche then to reunite with the other two parties (under Ed Hillary and Charles Evans) and then we split up again into three parties for the second acclimatisation run. John Hunt has decided to send a party on to the Khumbu icefall during this second period to explore it thoroughly and bash a route up it and bridge the crevasses in preparation for the big lift of food and equipment to advanced base in the Western Cwm. Ed and I are two of the select four chosen for this job and we're rather pleased (George Band and Mike Westmacott are the other two.)

It's practically dark and I must stop as I can't see what I'm writing. We're all fit and raring to go. There are lots of things to do – so much so that I've read nothing and written very few letters.

·

I haven't had any mail since Katmandu (6th March) and I'm looking forward to the next lot. Before I forget – Betty, could you hurry and send three tartan wool shirts to me at Katmandu. Several of the English boys want to get one – My size will do – Three different. I must stop, it's dark.

Cheers to all, George.

Thyangboche Meadow
6th April 1953

Dear Folks,

Another perfect day. This year the Everest district seems to specialise in them. You might wonder why we don't rush in and take a crack at the mountain? Here, at Thyangboche, the day is perfect and Everest is clear and sharp in the sky but a look through binoculars displays evidence of a wind slamming snow particles off the ridge and the cold up there in April would be unbearable.

The first of our two acclimatisation periods is over and our little party, for one, has had a great time. Eight days ago we broke into three groups and each went to explore a different and unmapped valley. Charles Evans took a party of four (Tom Bourdillon, Mike Westmacott and George Band) to the south of Ama Dablam, where they climbed to 19,500 ft getting used to the height and practising with both 'open' and 'closed' circuit oxygen. Charles had a photo-theodolite and did a lot of mapping photography with it. They all returned last night just after us.

Ed has a party up the Chola Kola valley and is due back today. They were to explore the Chola Kola, practise with open circuit oxygen and map the area. With him are Mike Ward, Wilfred Noyce and Charles Wylie. I was in John Hunt's party along with 'Greg' Gregory and Tenzing (the sirdar who went to 28,000 ft last year and is counted as one of the summit potentials).

We went up the Imja valley under the Lhotse-Nuptse wall (5 miles long and between 25,000 and 27,000 ft in height!) – and under the cliffs of Nuptse we discovered a glacier and a hidden peak which we climbed and called 'Chukung Peak' – it was just under 20,000 ft. This is briefly what we did.

We left here on 30th March – everybody carrying quite heavy loads (a theory of Hunt's with which I don't agree) and we camped at Dingboche – a village at 15,000 ft where the lama from this monastery was visiting to bless the yaks, ploughs, people, potatoes and fields at the spring planting. Lhotse dominates Dingboche – Lhotse is nearly 28,000 ft and is only three or four miles away and it seems to lean overhead – and that night the sunset on it and the streaming cloud from it, was exceedingly beautiful.

On 31st we saw the end of a glacier and went up it towards Nuptse and camped at 17,400 ft. For water we sent the Sherpas to cut blocks of ice from the glacier. April 1st was a memorable day. We all tried the 'open circuit' oxygen on a peak – an easy climb from 18,000 to 19,800 ft. The open circuit consists of a frame holding a big air-force oxygen cylinder holding 1,400 litres of pure oxygen at a pressure of 3,300 atmospheres. The bottle has a tap and a pressure gauge, then a breaking down valve which controls the flow and feeds it slowly into an 'economiser', a bag with an automatic valve which opens on breathing in and closes on breathing out; this avoids waste.

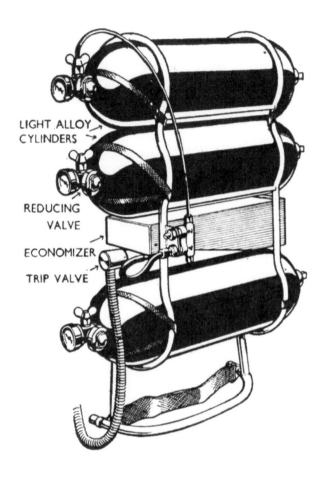

LIGHT ALLOY
CYLINDERS

REDUCING
VALVE

ECONOMIZER

TRIP VALVE

The open circuit apparatus allowed the climber to breathe air from the atmosphere as well as oxygen from the cylinders on the climber's back.

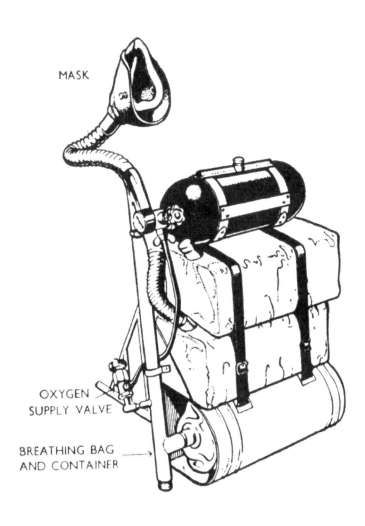

MASK

OXYGEN
SUPPLY VALVE

BREATHING BAG
AND CONTAINER

With the closed circuit, where no outside air entered the mask, the climber only used the cylinder oxygen, which after being breathed in and out could be used again.

From the economiser comes a tube which goes through a valve which can be adjusted to two flow rates (either 3 litres or 6 litres of oxygen per minute).

The tube then screws into a mask that we wear. The mask covers nose and mouth and is fitted with valves to allow air from outside the mask to come an as well as the puff of pure oxygen from the bottle. On breathing out the mask valves open and all expelled air goes out. This sounds a bit complicated – but it's an easy gadget compared with Tom Bourdillon's 'closed circuit' which has a very tight fitting mask which seals the breather off from the outside world. The inhaled breath is pure oxygen and the exhaled breath is breathed into a soda-lime canister which absorbs the carbon dioxide and uses the generated heat for warming the next breath!

Anyway on 1st April I tried the open circuit. It weighs 35 lbs which is a great disadvantage. I had walked up to 18,000 feet for the first time and was feeling pretty lethargic and slightly headachy and not in the slightest did I feel like pushing on to 19,800. However, with Tenzing I fitted on the mask and checked the gear, connected up and switched on. We set off together – each on 3 litres per minute and began swinging up-hill. Instead of puffing and panting I breathed deeply and evenly and stepped up without that feeling of fatigue that I have had before being acclimatised. It was a terrific relief to find the outfit really worked.

With every breath I felt the economiser give a little gasp and send a puff of gas into the mask. The tiny rubber valves in the mask flip-flopped with the breaths and I felt wonderful. With the mask and tube and goggled eyes Tenzing looked a rare specimen of the scientific age and I felt I did too.

We had been going for 25 minutes and had climbed some 500 feet when there was a sudden explosion and a roaring of air and I nearly fell over with fright. Tenzing was clawing at his frame – his reducing valve had blown out. He closed the tap on the bottle and took off his set and we saw that nothing we could do would fix it. He went down and I pushed on. I soon forgot the incident and began to marvel at the boost that the set was giving me. Whether it was so or not I don't know, but I had a feeling of rhythm and power with the oxygen flowing in. There was a very slight hiss from the bottle and the economiser puffed and sucked and the mask kept out the cold from my face. Drops of moisture dribbled out of the mask outlet and froze soon after they hit the ground. The top of the hill looked far away when I stopped to change the flow rate to six litres and I was amazed to find I got there in ten minutes. On six litres, I felt like running and could climb at sea-level pace.

On top at 19,800 feet I sat down, drank in the high flow rate and enjoyed the view. The view was familiar to me but I still enjoyed seeing Makalu, Cho Oyu, Gyachung Kang, Lhotse and co. and all the sharp impassable ice teeth further south of me. To save oxygen we had agreed to switch off on top and come down without it. I did this and coming down was not too bad. I noticed the weight, whereas before I hadn't. Coming down doesn't tax the breathing like going up.

John Hunt and Greg, and lastly Tenzing, did the same run with the good apparatus and we all did the 1,800 feet in about 1 hour – actually Tenzing did it in 50 minutes which for any altitude is really cracking along. He is very fit, a beautiful mover and very used to high altitudes. As well, he's an unspoiled character after

71

the publicity of his climbing. He's the ideal companion, with an infectious sense of humour and the desire to yodel and whoop like hell when he's happy (most unusual in a Tibetan). He speaks a little English and is teaching me Hindustani and a bit of Tibetan. He's everybody's favourite.

We were all excited by the success of the oxygen and with that and the newness to altitude I couldn't get to sleep. I took a sleeping pill as an experiment – the others use them almost regularly. I slept like a log for ten hours and had the most vivid dreams near waking. The only effect it had was to leave me slow for an hour and I had to force myself into action. I don't think I'll try any more!

On 2nd April we took a light camp to the head of the glacier and camped at 18,900 ft and on 3rd April climbed an ice peak which was just about 20,000 feet. John Hunt led this and cut steps up 400 feet of snow and occasional ice. He measured the slope with a clinometer – a steady angle of 51° which is steep. We traversed the peak and went down to our 17,400 camp.

On 4th we climbed to a pass at 20,000 feet hoping to cross into the Khumbu valley but found the far side an impossible cliff. We took a round of angles on all the trigged peaks – sketched in the new glaciers and returned the way we had come, getting back last night – fit and very satisfied with our first run to a moderate height. Here's a rough map.

Now we're feeding and resting at Thyangboche for 3 days before the second acclimatisation period begins (10 days). For this the parties are mixing up. Two parties are going off on slightly longer journeys while the third is going to reccy the Khumbu icefall to make a route up it before the main attack

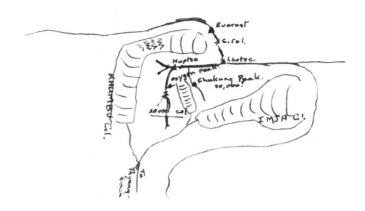

begins. For this Ed and I have been chosen with George Band (the wireless and food officer) and Mike Westmacott (ex-army engineer and in charge of the crevasse bridging and tackle) to help us. Like Ed I'm looking forward to this next bout as it's right in our line of amusement. So far the winter has been unusually dry and snowless, which may mean that the icefall is more broken, icy and difficult than after heavy falls.

Everest is quite snowy now – while we were away, a fall covered all the high peaks and the wind is now busy clearing it away.

Although mail-runners are going out, none have yet come in and we are expecting the first delivery about 18th April which seems to be a long way off. After the 20th April the long job of placing camps and supplies on Everest will begin in preparation for an assault on or after 15th May. We are all hoping that this is the year. I wonder what you're all doing for Easter? Kindest regards to all. I hope the club had a fine Easter jaunt – as I did!

George.

P.S. As from 1st May until June 6th the B.B.C. and All India radio (Delhi) will be broadcasting a special weather bulletin for us to tell of the approach of monsoon. You may hear but I think it will probably be after midnight. All India (Delhi) – 17 hrs. 18 minutes (Indian time). B.B.C. 14 hrs. 15 minutes. 6½ behind you. (G.M.T.).

Geo.

Camp II
16th April 1953

Dear Folks,

A few hours ago, Ed Hillary, George Band and I established Camp II. What a place! What a wind! What a view – if you can get outside against the wind! It has taken four days to make a route through to here. We established Base and then Camp I at the foot of the icefall on 12th April. The night temperatures on the glacier have been around 30° to 35° of frost, and the nights have been wonderfully starlit. All night the glacier splits and cracks and booms – I know because I spent much of the first two nights awake and often out of the tent with a violent attack of diarrhoea. For three days I ate nothing and life was grim. During this time, Ed, George B. and Mike Westmacott attacked the icefall. From below it looked exceedingly broken and I watched them with binoculars. Most of the time they were out of sight behind towers, blocks and along crevasse ledges. They returned both nights with hair-raising accounts of the difficulty – and danger. Ed says that it's far more broken than 1951 and the Sherpas say the Swiss found it better than this.

On the third day I joined Ed and George B. while Mike Westmacott went sick. We tried a new line near the centre of the icefall and for a thousand feet made steep but safe progress and then we hit a crumbling shattered area, where huge blocks rocked and toppled on touch. We went on until a huge serac hung over the only route like a great combing wave. We decided the original route was better and today we carried up our bedding while three Sherpas carried the primus stove, two Meade tents, a walkie-talkie wireless (9 lbs) and two days food. I was really impressed with the route, which contains 'Mike's Horror' and 'Hillary's Horror' – two ticklish sections which each overcame on the reconnaissance of the route. The upper part is very shattered and rather menaced by overhanging ice and just below this tiny safe area where we have the tents there has been a subsidence since yesterday.

As I came up to this place I saw that yesterday's tracks ended at a crevasse lip. I stepped back off the lip, which looked solid, and gave it a heavy belt with the axe to hear for possible creaks, when the whole thing about 8 feet long and 3 feet wide dropped away at my feet and left me with the back spikes of my crampons holding the firm lip. After two hours in the icefall we were keyed for this and apart from one widening crevasse, which took a running leap, we reached here about 2 p.m.

Ahead of us there appears a tremendous tangle of cliffs and towers and we wonder if we'll get a route through to the Western Cwm tomorrow. We begin to realise now why the Swiss got into the Cwm (pronounced <u>Coom</u>) last year and stayed there until their attempt ran down. There's no getting away from it, the Khumbu icefall is a nasty spot.

At 5 p.m. we are going to call up base on the walkie-talkie phone. If this works it will be invaluable. It consists of a box little bigger than a telephone with a telephone mouth-piece and an earphone. Three light batteries are plugged into the box – a light 6 ft spring steel aerial is plugged in and you're away. With fixed frequency, you merely switch on the power, push a button to speak and release it to listen. So far they have worked wonderfully well.

We also have an ordinary receiving set with which to receive the weather broadcasts from B.B.C. and All India Radio during May. We have had this set at Base Camp and each night we listen to Ceylon and get an English programme. Last night it was Hawaiian, then light Opera and a Tommy Dorsey programme. The Sherpas all come into our tent and listen with big grins and we join in the songs we know and throw off at their commercial advertising. At 7.30 we usually switch to Moscow and hear their version of the world news.

I'm cook tonight and soon I'll have to set the primus roaring to hot up the stewed steak (tinned) and peas – with packeted asparagus soup – followed by tinned fruit cake and coffee. It sounds good but up here it doesn't cook anything like sea-level and we are starting to talk of home cooking.

In a day or two we hope to get our first mail delivery and we're all hanging back on letters waiting for this delivery – which will be our first for over 6 weeks.

More anon, George.

Lake Camp
19th April 1953

Although stony, windy and dusty, Lake Camp is at present a warm paradise with a ring of wonderful mountain scenery. The avalanches are just occasional rumbles and now that the first mail delivery has arrived the world is a peaceful, pleasant place. Two days ago it wasn't! The 17th April (isn't that Dad's birthday?) was a nerve-wracking day – the day that Ed, George Band and I reccied the top section of the Khumbu icefall and finally peeped into the Cwm.

The night had been very gusty and the morning was bleak with cloud around Pumori, Lingtren, Nuptse and Everest. The wind blew at different velocities at different levels. It was most noisy over the Lho La, which was five hundred feet above us. The speed there was terrific and it moaned and surged just as if surf. We wirelessed to Base to say we were setting out and left at 8.15, heavily clothed and all tastefully covered in royal blue windproof suits. Our spirits were high and apart from a few heart-in-the-mouth moments we stayed on top all day.

The view upwards from Camp II was not reassuring – a mass of blocks, debris and seracs, standing amongst a good thousand feet of twisted icefall. None of us had done anything like this before and we knew we'd be impressed. We spent 4 hours getting through most of it, winding over, through and round a great cemetery of rubble. At one time we wound too far to the right and stopped under great cliffs hanging off Nuptse. A long traverse left and we finished under a 60 ft barrier that cut us from the easier slopes leading into the Cwm.

We pushed sideways through a deep cleft that felt like sneaking through the jaws of a clam. The two walls tilted inwards and one, although a 30 foot chunk, did not feel too stable. Finally after much inspection and searching we found a way onto the great block with the vertical walls. Ed led this magnificently – first up a face, then a 30 foot diagonal ice crack which finished in an overhang – but with a lot of grunting and scratching with his crampons he got inside and wriggled up and over the last 9 feet and there we were looking into the Cwm, but with still another 60 foot block to get up. The wind here was terrific – we were above the Lho La level and when the big gusts roared we just had to whack the axe in and crouch down. Both George and I were pretty tired by this time, although Ed seemed inexhaustible. We returned to camp, rushing the most dangerous bits and occasionally pointing out to each other a Swiss flag – left waving, torn and faded on the bamboo wands that they placed to mark out their Autumn route. The continuity of their route is quite gone – here and there on an inaccessible block with 40 foot walls all around is a Swiss flag like a surrealist's dream of a golf course. We too are marking our route with bamboo wands and flags – the Swiss flags were maroon and advertised 'Bally Boots' – ours are plain yellow and orange squares.

Just before we reached Camp II, John Hunt came up with a Sherpa to get a first hand impression of our route. He was very impressed with our efforts and we enjoyed the pat on the back. We all descended to Camp I and then yesterday to Lake Camp for a couple of days rest. The mail had arrived, and we fell on it desperately. We swapped news until late in the night and even at 2 a.m. I was tossing and staring at the tent roof thinking over the news in the letters, too excited to sleep after the big day on the icefall. I noticed, too, that Ed on one side and George Band on the other were lying sleepless too. The 17th April had been quite a day.

Tomorrow Ed, George Band and I are setting out for Camp II again to flag and cut the most likely route through to Camp III on top of the last great block. For the last block we are going to fix a 35 foot rope-ladder. While we're doing this, others will be improving the route to Camp II with wooden logs and aluminium ladders across the worst sections (especially 'Hillary's Horror' and 'Hell Fire Alley') and then about 26th April the long and tedious business of load-carrying begins. All trips through the icefall will have to be escorted by one of the European party – I am in the first High Altitude team to relay loads from Camp III to IV and then to V at the foot of the Lhotse Face. Wilf Noyce is my companion, while six others with 21 Sherpas relay from Camp I through the icefall to Camp III. Ed, John Hunt and Charles Evans are going ahead then to reccy up the Lhotse Face.

The assault oxygen – 57 bottles in light alloy – has just arrived in Thyangboche by special delivery from England and will be here for packing up in 3 or 4 days. These bottles were left till the last possible moment to ensure that they arrived with the maximum pressure. With 1,600 litres at 3,300 atmospheres pressure leaks are very difficult to avoid. With the first lot that we used in practise and training – held in the usual R.A.F. cylinders – the loss through leakage en route was nearly one third. If that happens to the assault bottles it will be a major disaster.

Guess that's all – the next two weeks I shall be high in the Cwm and probably letter writing will be at a minimum.

Cheers, George.

Base Camp
25th April 1953

Dear Betty,

This just contains odds and ends. Some stamps from odd countries; a cutting from a London paper – a rival of the 'Times'. Here is quite a story :– The 'Times' have a copyright of all the news we send them, but there's no rules about news if the rival paper sends a special correspondent and that is what the 'Daily Telegraph' did. A Ralph Izzard came specially to Katmandu to pirate the story which he did most successfully. At Badgaon – where we collected our 300 coolies and left on the march he snooped around with his camera and several stooges who found out all they could. He printed a story about Tenzing – our sirdar – which made everybody mad.

The outcome was that he beat the 'Times' to the story and pictures of the expedition departure and now the 'Times' have flown out a special correspondent who has just arrived here at Base Camp – but not before Izzard – who with commendable enterprise got permission to enter Nepal and in light boots and very little gear arrived at Base camp <u>a week ago</u>. Here he took photographs and snooped around – saw our wireless sets and headed off with his story and the intention to get a powerful wireless so that he can tap our mountain messages and wireless them ahead of the 'Times' to London. To counter this the 'Times' have devised a code name for all of us and all our camps have code names which we use when wirelessing. Real cloak and dagger stuff. It's amusing to us – but dead serious for the correspondents.

We are all on the side of the 'Times', but even when we send

On 12 April, George and Ed found the site for Base Camp, surrounded by huge pinnacles of Khumbu glacier ice. Within 10 days the whole expedition's stores and equipment were here.

George Band leads a Sherpa team through the icefall ferrying stores up the mountain.

After another exhausting day on the icefall, Ed enjoys a New Zealand newspaper that was sent to George with a bundle of letters from home.

them outstanding photographs they don't print them – which annoys us somewhat.

These photographs include one of Ed who was turning round belligerently to say "If you don't get the hell out of here I'll kick your backside!" and there Izzard snapped him.

The third enclosure is a piece of brown paper that rolled the 'Weekly News' – thanks for the Weekly it was very popular with everybody and it was very homely I thought. Took me right back home. A scribbled advertisement of Dads arriving all the way on Everest – so I'll send it home just for the ride.

George Band is just calling up Camps II and III on the walkie-talkie at our 8 a.m. call and I have to pay the mail-runner and send him off on his month's round trip to Katmandu.

Today and for the next 2 weeks we are packing stores up to Camp IV – advanced base on Everest at 23,000 ft. After that, expect an attempt any time.

Cheers, George.

CHAPTER THREE

Base Camp
29th April 1953

Dear Folks,

After the bout of sickness I've recovered rapidly and have been on the 'bus run' up to Camp III with a train of Sherpas carrying loads. While I was on the sick list here (4 days) I was packing high altitude rations and then one day the yak arrived. We had ordered a yak (cost 120 rupees) to be driven up the glacier and killed at base camp. It was a shock to me when the yak arrived to be named expedition butcher and asked to do the deed. A yak!

None of the Sherpas would kill it and so we produced a .22 rifle and I sharpened a pocket knife, a sheath knife of Tom Stobart's and a kukri. Then armed to the teeth and with George Band holding the yak on a 30 ft rope we went to the kill. The yak guessed some evil and began to perform. George B. did a smart circle round an ice tower and hung on but the yak snapped this off and then the glacier took on the look of a rodeo. I planted the knives and began to stalk – avoiding getting a watching Sherpa – or cavorting George and Tom S. who was shouting directions from a distance (he has filmed big game hunting in Kenya!) – these people were in imminent danger of death. I crept in close and put a shot between the ear and eye and then waited for the yak to drop dead.

Not a bit. It began bleeding from the mouth and with a baleful look charged at me. I dropped the gun and leapt to the rope with George and together we circled an ice tower and tried to tie the beast up short and cut its throat. As we wrapped the rope round the tower the yak followed and we raised yells of encouragement as we ran round and round. Then the yak gave a heave and so did we – and the ice tower broke. Then the fun really began. We headed off for another tower and the yak followed and we dodged and leapt scything down a whole forest of four foot pinnacles. Tom S. planted a hasty shot between us and into the yak's neck and the fun began again. Finally, we anchored round a big tower and the yak tired and I grabbed the rifle and from 15 yards or so put a shot near the eye and the poor beast dropped like a log. The Sherpas were up hill – at a safe distance – clicking their tongues at the inexperience and cruel handling done by the sahibs while George B. with torn hands and Tom S. still from a safe distance panted with me after the kill. We didn't feel very pleased with our efforts but without more ado cut the poor yak's throat and with inadequate tools set about skinning it. This was quite a smooth job and in 2 hours we had a gutted carcase and with a kukri cut it into legs, necks, steaks and the usual butchers shapes and hung it in an ice cave. There was only 200 lbs. of meat in the carcase – which is surprising considering a yak is as big as a small cow. In five days we have nearly finished the whole thing. We've had liver, brains, kidneys, heart (stuffed) and now the muscle meat, which even after 40 minutes in the pressure cooker is tough.

Next meat order is five sheep instead of a yak (sheep is 23 rupees – rupee = 1/6) and I'm the local butcher. When I get home I am going to take a few more lessons from Dad – real ones instead of just watching – and I'm hoping to have something better than a 3 bob pocket knife and a piece of stone for a steel.

Tomorrow Ed and I are to take the Sherpa team on the two-day carry to Camp III. For the past 10 days Sherpas – escorted by sahibs (that's us!) have been making daily carries up the icefall to Camp III where another team is busy carrying loads on to Camp IV at 22,000 feet in the Western Cwm.

Tomorrow I'll try and give you an impression of the carry to Camp II and III. I've been up several times now and the trip is just a grind now that the route is made easy. I told you of our first trips up the icefall and how difficult it was. Now with wooden poles across the worst crevasses and fixed ropes to swing up and down the ice cliffs, a duralium bridge across the worst crevasse and a 35 ft rope ladder up the final ice-wall (which we climbed by a difficult ice-crack) the route now assumes a steady crampon plod up 2,000 feet of icefall winding in and out among towers and seracs following a line of 90 marker flags.

Still the route is not without daily serac falls, the odd Sherpa falling through a bridge and saved by the rope – the noticeable widening of some cracks and the subsidence of one section we call the 'atom bomb' area. We have names for all the tricky bits – 'Hillary's

Horror' is now bridged and has a fixed rope up the ice cliff – after that comes the 'hell-fire alley' then 'atom bomb', 'jump crevasse' and Camp II. Above Camp II is 'ledge ice cliff' 'bloody crevasse', 'boulder alley', 'the nut-cracker', 'the ladder' and Camp III.

Camp III is about 20,000 feet on top of the last great blocks of ice at the top of the icefall. After that you cross a big 16 ft bridge (duralium) and wind along a level crevassed glacier for three miles to Camp IV, 22,000 ft near the Lhotse Face.

In three days time the most crucial tests of all will be made. Charles Evans, Tom Bourdillon, Charles Wylie and Mike Westmacott will be setting off for Camp IV with oxygen sets – both closed circuit and open circuit – to attempt the Lhotse Face and place Camps V and VI, and try to reach South Col on oxygen.

The Lhotse Face looks icy and is our next big problem and the big test is – how will the closed and open circuit go at high altitude? If the closed circuit works it will be an absolute winner – it enables the climber to go at nearly sea level pace and for 12 hours (we hope) without great fatigue. If this is so a really strong attempt will be able to be put in. The open circuit is not so useful at high altitudes as the higher you go the less efficient it becomes. On this test on the Lhotse Face (25,000 ft) the planning of the final assault rests. We are all looking forward to some definite conclusions on this oxygen question. We have a feeling that these four might well be a 'sacrificial party'. The effort they put in in testing the apparatus may well exhaust them and prevent them from being effective in the final assault. Whatever happens – nearly everyone will be needed for the final lift of stores as high as we can get for the launching of the final team. A ridge camp (at

The first tent at Camp III was established on 22 April at the entrance to the Western Cwm. Westmacott looks up towards the formidable Lhotse Face.

The icefall was a frozen cascade of giant ice blocks, constantly moving and changing, pouring in waves towards Base Camp.

27,500 or 28,000?) is still planned and this will burn out two or three of us as well.

Still the final assault plan is still in the melting pot. Naturally we all hope to be one of the final pair, but realise that can't be so. Still I hope I'm fit enough to get to the South Col or above and I'll feel I've done my bit.

We're hoping for another mail-runner tomorrow or the next day and when the runner arrives Base Camp takes on a gala air and everyone is full of home spirits. This is a wonderfully happy party – due mainly to the generalship of John Hunt who contrives to keep everyone busy and pushing together for the top in a solid bunch. He is a wonderful leader. All the boys are excellent types, easy to get along with and most useful anywhere on a mountain.

I've got a strong feeling that if the weather is slightly kind this will be the last and successful Everest Expedition.

More anon, George.

Rest Camp
4th May 1953

You'll excuse this miserly use of paper I hope! On 1st May three of us established this camp three hours below the Base Camp (which is on a moraine patch on the ice at the foot of the icefall) and here, at a place the locals call Loje, we have a tent on the grass and there are a few tiny flowers growing in the shelter of a rock. These flowers are brave and persistent because each day (even here at 16,500 ft) for the past 23 days we have had afternoon snowfalls and odd thunder-showers that cover the ground with hail stones.

This is the season of "Westerly Disturbances" which precede the monsoon and they have been so persistent that since the 13th April we have had snow every afternoon. This snow is making the work above Camp III very tedious and heart-breaking. Every day the wind and snow fills the tracks which have to be remade.

Yesterday Ed come down here with Mike Westmacott. Ed had news of the closed circuit oxygen and his test run on open circuit.

On 30th April John Hunt, Charles Evans and Tom Bourdillon went up to Camp IV on closed circuit to place Camps V and VI and try to get to South Col and test the closed circuit. Mike Ward (the doctor) and Charles Wylie went up on open circuit to back up.

On 2nd May Ed and Tenzing did a run on open circuit from Base to Camp IV to see if this gave them any real benefit. Ed arrived here yesterday and reported that the open circuit was "bloody marvellous". They went to Camp IV and back from Base in the day and arrived tired but not exhausted as anyone would on no oxygen. Their times. They left:

> 6.30 from Base 18,000 ft.
> 8.00 at Camp II 19,500 ft.
> 8.50 at Camp III 20,500 ft.
> 10.50 at Camp IV 22,000+ ft.

This is a terrific set of times as normally we go to:

> Camp II the first day in 3 hours and rest
> Camp III the second day in 2½ hours and rest
> Camp IV the third day in 3½ hours and rest and the descent can be made in one day. They came down the same afternoon in a great blizzard.

They waited at Camp IV for the return of the Lhotse Face reccy on the 2nd and they all came down to Camp IV quite done in. The closed circuit produces a lot of heat and they were terribly handicapped by the sweating and heat that enveloped them. The weight of the closed circuit is much greater – about 40 lbs and this they found at 23,000+ was an exhausting factor. The open circuit with a light alloy cylinder will give 3 hours supply at 4 litres per minute. Weight only 18 lbs, a negligible weight for the advantage it gives. And if bottles can be spread between camps the open circuit may be the best set to use. But we will have to await the results of the full closed circuit tests. The closed circuit reccy boys told Ed that the Lhotse Face climb was far more difficult than they had anticipated – and now the reccy aim was not to get above the South Col but merely to reach and place Camp VI on the Lhotse Face.

The Lhotse Face will require many days work before loads can be lifted to the South Col. A lot of steps will have to be cut (how? at 25,000 feet), several fixed ropes put on the traverse to the South Col and the route marked with bamboo poles and flags.

The next letters will probably be staccato affairs from Camp IV or above as I expect to go up on to the Lhotse Face in the next week. By the time you get this the final shot for the summit will probably have been made. I wonder what the outcome will be?

We've been here 3 days now and everyday we've been expecting the Dak Wallah (mail-runner). Each day we've walked down the track and looked down the valley for the two scraggy figures that carry our bag to Katmandu and back. The round trip takes nearly a month. Yesterday we really expected him and the whole day went by and he hadn't come. Snow began, lightning and then the Sherpas served up by kerosene lamp our yak stew. Stew was half finished and we were all disgruntled and angry at the Dak runner. Talk grew rough and threatening. Someone muttered – "The rotten bugger is probably sitting out of the snow", another, "Lazy bastard's drinking chang in the lower villages", another "He's three days overdue now, I wonder if snow has blocked the route? He needs a good kick in the arse and I'm just the one to give it to him."

Then at dusk, cold, snowing and really bleak, the Dak runner pushed his head in the tent with a toothy grin, powdered with snow and pinched with cold. "Salaam Sahib!" – "The Dak Wallah! Hooray!"

"Shabash" (the Hindi for 'well done') and our anger was melted. All threats forgotten in the surprise and pleasure he brought. We slapped his shoulder and smiled at him – and began sorting the bundle of letters, joking and throwing off at one another if we thought the handwriting on the cover was from a girl.

The arrival of the Dak Wallah at the expedition base is a great occasion. Now with <u>16</u> letters I'm as happy as a sand-boy. I haven't a hope of answering them all before I go back up hill – but I'll have them to sort over and re-read and answer, I hope, in the tired times at the end of a high camp day.

[Dear Mother, Please excuse the direct reporting of this account. We're not bad at heart, but that is how it is in verbatim speech. It seems much worse in writing, but to clear out the profanity would make the account untrue. Still, perhaps we shouldn't write all the things that happen!]

I am slightly worried about the cyclostyling of my letters. The circulation is wide and may tempt someone to publish bits.

Could a note about this be appended to the reproduction? The consequences are rather severe – a personal account to the 'Times' and a £1,000 fine to the expedition.

The local joke here is on Griff Pugh, the physiologist, an absent minded scientist who was going up to Camp IV to observe the effects of oxygen and oxygen lack on the reccy party. He set off with a box that he thought included his apparatus for alveoli samples and various air tests. The first day he just reached Camp II. The second day he got to Camp III with a great struggle and suffering from altitude. He had occasion to check his gear and found that his physiological box was not what he thought – it was an identical box that was filled with bottles of chutney! Griff came down then without doing his experiments and rather suspicious that someone organised the swap.

More anon, George.

Camp III
8th May 1953

Dear Folks,

For a day or two I am based alone, with 14 'high altitude' Sherpas doing the load lift to Camp IV. Camp IV is to be our Advanced Base in the Western Cwm – it's approx 22,000 ft and III is about 20,500 ft. I came up here a few days ago to run the Cwm lift with George Band. George did the lift on the 6th – a fairly tough day and then went sick with sore throat, cold and a bit of altitude. He lay up yesterday and did not improve so went down with the 'low altitude' Sherpas today.

I should explain our set-up. A separate Sherpa team of 14 escorted by Sahibs works from Base Camp (18,000) up to Camp II (19,500) the first day and up to Camp III (20,500) and down to Base the second day. These are L.A. (low altitude teams).

The H.A. team (high altitude) works from Camp III (20,500) to Camp IV (22,000) and does the trip every day escorted by a Sahib. Tomorrow the H.A. will split and one team will work III to IV and another under Ed Hillary will work IV to V (Camp V is at 23,000 ft at the foot of the Lhotse Face). The L.A. escort is the one everyone dislikes but has to take several turns. I've done 4 or 5 and done my share. It consists, as I said before in one letter, of a nerve-racking two days in the ice-fall and lately several serac falls have spewed over the route and several more logs are needed over widening crevasses – [*This isn't a line. I've just had to have the ink bottle thawed over the primus to fill my pen – I had it in my boot thinking it may have escaped the cold – temperatures at night here are recorded at -30°F. It's 2 p.m. now after a hot day!*]

When I came up to III the other day I came up with 'Greg' who is escorting L.A. teams at the moment. About 7.30 a.m. at II on 6th the glacier gave a terrific crack and just outside the tent a crack of over a foot opened and just below camp there was a subsidence over 100 yards area. This is the first time I've ever seen a sudden move in an icefall – and we realise now how the 'Atom Bomb' area below II changes so often and is so unstable. The 'Atom Bomb' is a shattered, fairly level area that wobbles when you walk on it, and odd falling blocks drop hundreds of feet and then rumble and shake the whole mass. Easily one of the most eerie places ever.

Advance Base at Camp IV was established in early May, about a mile from the foot of the Lhotse Face.

A Sherpa team moves supplies up through the icefall. They are crossing the ladder bridge at 'Nasty Crevasse' just above Camp II.

Everyone likes the release from L.A. run, and I was really glad when John put me in charge of the build-up to IV and V. Yesterday was my first day. What a day, what a thrashing we got. I had 13 Sherpas with 45 lb loads – 5 oxygen (soda lime canisters, one open circuit set, several light alloy cylinders, 11 lbs with 850 litres at 2,800 atmospheres) and a few R.A.F. cylinders (20 lbs with 1,400 litres at 3,300 atmospheres), several boxes of composite army ration, 2 boxes high altitude ration, 6 manilla ropes for Lhotse Face fixed ropes, 7 gallons kerosene and one gal. meths. – it sounds a lot, but it is but a fraction of the <u>2½ tons</u> that we are expecting to put there!

Every afternoon we've had snow and the weather report from India told us that a depression was following the westerly disturbance. On 6th May it snowed heavily as George Band came down and snowed most of the night. However with a struggle I got the Sherpas loaded and away on 7th at 8 a.m. The snow was 15 to 18 inches deep, and I plugged trail for them. At 9.30 it began to snow. We had crossed the 18 ft crevasse by the duralium bridge (we should get a good photo of this – I think it's the same one the Swiss had trouble with – it's very sensational looking into the depth between the ladder rungs – we all crawl and are thankful for the four leg position). Soon after the 18 ft crevasse is another that you have to go down into and out the other side. After that the route is a long winding walk back and forwards across the crevasses, gradually climbing, until there is a straight forward grind up the last mile to IV. The route is marked with flags on 4 ft bamboo poles every 60 yards and every crevasse crossing.

From 9.30 a.m. the snow fell heavily and I thought I was well nigh exhausted when IV appeared in the mist at noon. I had been plugged in calf-deep snow without a real halt and I welcomed the idea of following the four ropes of Sherpas back to camp. We had only 10 minutes there and they set off down the deep rut of our up route at a great pace. The snow increased and wind began to drift the top powder. After the first mile the tracks had completely gone and the weather was so thick that the flags disappeared. The Sherpas naturally looked to me and I began plugging again searching for the flags, unable to see the line of crevasses even ten feet away. I grew desperately tired – everybody was covered with ice and glued into haggard expressions by the cold. Things were grim when Topky on my rope went through a huge masked crevasse. He didn't go more than three feet but was scared considerably – so was I.

For a while we couldn't get the next flag and soft snow avalanches were pouring into the mist about 40 yards to my left. Immediately right was a great crevasse and the Sherpas were near to panic. I began thinking of Captain Scott and his plight – and thought what a bleak time he must have had. Kunsha saw the next flag and we took a long time to reach it with snow now nearly knee deep. No one suggested a spell but we all lay round the flag as if it were a rest centre and shelter. The snow lifted later and we sighted the next flag and recalling the lay of the country we flogged on and crossed the down and up crevasse, the bridge, and although it was from there about 400 yards to camp it took us quarter of an hour. It was 4 p.m., the snow was lifting slightly, as we fell into the tents.

We were all so flogged that we requested a rest day today – and by wireless John ordered a complete rest and requested that George Band descend and recuperate. John and Ed will be up today to relieve me on this lift while I go ahead to V with two Sherpas to cut steps and fix ropes on the Lhotse Face above and below Camp VI and shift the site of VI to the Swiss camp VI, about 24,500 feet.

Tom Stobart, our cameraman, came up here last week but felt ill after one night and went down. The doctors were in the Cwm at the time and didn't see him for three days and when they did inspect him they confirmed that he was already recovering from pneumonia! Poor Tom, he was very ill and will be a week before he gets about again. In the meantime I have been getting as much movie stuff as I can and I'm sure I've got some good shots of the icefall route between Base and III. I shall be lugging a light 16 mm. colour camera up to IV, V and VI and hope I have the energy and clearness of mind to get a record of the Lhotse Face work. Up here, although you think you're smart, you continually forget to correct the lens stop as the light changes – or alter the focus after a close-up shot. All little things that you think you'd never forget. Even when well acclimatised to this height the lack of oxygen shows itself in many little ways.

I am including one of John Hunt's Memos. It illustrates how energetic and careful he is in planning. For every change of plan and every camp there is a stream of written orders that are clear and appreciated. He has his mind on everything and everybody. He is easily the most conscientious man that ever led an expedition. We think he's amazing – if organisation counts for anything Everest is already conquered. I hope John is the leader of the successful team – he's certainly deserved it. He makes everyone else rest and conserve themselves – but never does himself.

John and Ed will soon be here and I must check the loads for tomorrow and see that the tea is ready for them. It's snowing again now – it has done so every afternoon since <u>12th April</u>! I wonder if it will stop for the attempt.

The Lhotse Face will take at least a fortnight from now – I think anyway – so the 'big crack' won't be for a while yet.

More anon – John will be telling me tonight of the detailed assault plan – on closed and open circuit oxygen.

Cheers to all, George.

**Camp VI, 23,500 ft
15th May 1953**

Dear Betty,

There is such a lot to say and such a lot been doing in these five days that I'll never be able to capture it all. Ed is going to take this to Camp V soon and from there I expect it will eventually filter through.

The big moment has arrived – the plans are announced and the date is set. The big move begins on the 20th May. Let me work downwards. The summit pair on open circuit oxygen are Ed and Tenzing, backed up to Ridge Camp, to be placed as near 28,000 ft by John Hunt and 'Greg' Gregory with five Sherpas all using open circuit oxygen who will then descend leaving Ed and Tenzing to spend the night and make the attempt. The day before Ed and Tenzing leave the South Col, Charles Evans and Tom Bourdillon on closed circuit will make a reccy from the South Col to South Summit and beyond if their oxygen and strength lasts. They are to report to summit party on the conditions above South Summit.

The carry to S. Col will be made by 14 Sherpas escorted first by Wilf Noyce, on open circuit and next day by Charles Wylie on open circuit. Where does George fit in? By that time I'm supposed to be exhausted having spent a week making a route up the Lhotse Face without oxygen – I'm halfway through the job now and still going strong (I hope) on the most terrific ice-climbing I've ever done.

The crux of the whole matter is the climbing of the Lhotse Face which leads to S. Col. This face was at first taken too cheaply and two or three days were allowed for the climbing and placing of Camp VI. Now Camp VI is established and Camp VII, some 12-1500 ft above and we still have a good thousand feet to go to the South Col.

The Lhotse Face was such a tough problem that to use any of the potential summit or S. Col team that the chances were great of exhausting them. That's where I came in – an expendable quantity with Mike Westmacott and George Band to make a route up the Lhotse Face without oxygen to prepare the way for the assault parties.

Camp VII, 24,600 ft
18th May 1953

Everything is moving so swiftly and the times for writing are so short that I can only summarise my doings. My doings have been the spearhead of the assault for the last week, and if I jot down roughly the day to day I may catch up something. I haven't written a diary even, so I'll try to catch up here.

Sunday, 10th May. To Camp IV with John and Ed and 19 Sherpas. A wonderful morning and did a lot of movie work among the crevasses. Snow began at midday, but after tea and talk I took four Sherpas on to Camp V which we occupied for the first time. With us we had 400 ft Beales line and 30 pitons and piton hammers to fix ropes on the Lhotse Face. The Sherpas I had were good, Da Tenzing, Ang Nima, Ang Namgyl, Gylgen. During the evening meal (Swiss biscuits, cheese and pemmican soup), I told them our job was to make an excellent route up the Lhotse Face and carry and place Camp VI as high as we could get it.

Da Tenzing made an impassioned speech in Hindustani with the other boys giving frequent "Here here's". He said, "With Sahib in front we will smash a route up the hardest places and we Sherpas will help until we drop – we will carry loads and stamp and cut until a wonderful route is made to the S. Col – then after five days we will all be "cuttum hogin" ('had it') and we will collapse at Base and rest and rest and rest, while the others go to the top." – "But what if I fall sick, or the altitude gets me?" "Nay Sahib, will be all right – if not we will kick him and push and pull him until the route is good – in five days all will be finished."

It was quite a session parliamentary – old Da Tenzing is a wonderful character, voluble and expressive with his hands and after this everyone felt the Lhotse Face was done! Little did we know!

It blew and snowed heavily that night – in fact snow has fallen daily since <u>April 11th until May 14th</u>. It is quite impossible to imagine what a handicap this daily snow is, and how every day climbing after fresh snow makes the going tedious.

On 11th May I set off with Ang Nima, with Da Tenzing, Ang Namgyl and Gylgen to follow later with our bedding, food and chattels. Gylgen suffered badly from altitude headache (we were at 23,000 ft) I gave him A.P.C. and he gamely came on later. Ang Nima and I plugged off from V and at 11 a.m. struck the first steep ice pitch and found a Swiss fixed rope there. I cut up this, but at midday it began to snow. We cut and cut up ice walls and over bulges and finally at 3 p.m. we came to the foot of some very steep cliffs and found again a Swiss fixed rope. It was too steep to climb without step cutting and taking turns we slugged on – soaked with snow, cold and desperately tired. The rope was 400 ft long and anchored every 50 ft by ice pitons. It was the steepest ice climbing I had been on and finally we came to a tiny ledge and pitched a tent and called it Camp VI. The three Sherpas followed us up valiantly, and while Ang Nima and I sagged in the tent they went back to V.

We slept like logs and were late away on the 12th (9.30 a.m.) – which brought a sharp note about early starts from John. From VI we pushed up only about 800 ft in four hours. The snow was knee and thigh deep in drifts and between were ice walls of hard green and blue ice. We cut several hundred steps and fixed four ropes with pitons and went down. The view from VI was superb and the evening, clearing after snow, showed us the jagged top of Nuptse (someone said "like a razor blade looked at through a microscope"). Pumori was level with us – Cho Oyu and Gyachung Kang were there too! I tried to photograph it but it was smack into the evening sun. The tent platform was so small that we could just anchor the guy ropes into the ice wall. A platform of snow 3 ft x 3 ft was all that was flat outside the tent opening. The 400 ft fixed rope was anchored under the tent and climbing began one step from the door!

On 13th John said he was coming up (wireless communication every day at 5 p.m.) to see the progress and would we improve the route downwards. We started step cutting from the door at 9 a.m. and in four hours had a wonderful stairway down the 400 ft of fixed rope. Most of the ice angle is agreed by all as over 50°. John announced his proximity by screaming from below, "Stop that cutting or you'll kill us!" We sat and waited and he arrived with every sign of extreme exhaustion and I sat with the movie camera taking an 8 second burst every now and then, as he laboured up until his twisted face filled the whole view-finder. As I filmed, scuds of wind-blown snow swept over him and I hope it will film as it really was. (It's wireless time, 5 p.m., and I must report our day's doings to Advanced Base) – The wireless was a cold session, because the aerial is attached to the box and has to be outside the tent and now a full gale is blowing.

John told me as he arrived on 13th that he had mail for me. "At least, I have some newspapers and Mike has the letters. Mike's buggered, I think you had better go down to him." Mike Westmacott was making his third valiant attempt to reach VI and each day the altitude stopped him. I went down and Mike was 300 ft below me. I had 200 ft of rope and shouted to him to reach the rope and we'd pull up the letters and Da Tenzing's load. It was an hour before Mike could reach the rope, tie on and we had his load. I took a hurried glance and saw a tiny canvas bag with a dozen letters and I whooped – it was easily the strangest mail delivery I'd had and we dragged back to VI loaded with rope, pitons, oxygen cylinders and letters.

It took over two hours to rush through the letters. A long one from Reuben – a wonderful surprise in which he said, "Something to read at 15 or 20,000 ft" – I was at 23,500, then my highest ever. There was a 'Free Lance' from Betty and a letter – she's never missed a mail yet – Geoff Milne, Pat Thorsby, Helen McKenzie, Prof. Finch – oh, and lots more, a bundle of newspapers from London, a Geographic Magazine – all of which is here with me now at VII – at about 25,000 ft. I was hoping to answer all the senders but I haven't had a chance since as every day has been terrific.

On 14th May Ang Nima and I left VI at 8.30 a.m. determined to get to Swiss VII and fix the route. The wind was bad that day and my feet froze badly – we were caked with ice and the cold air gave us very sore throats. The snow was wind-crusted and therefore easier. In four hours we reached the site of VII and sank down. The height is about 24,800 ft. We fixed several ropes on the steepest and most exposed parts and went down. The heat in the tent at VI was over 120°F and we nearly fainted. We both lay from 3 till 5 p.m. in complete exhaustion and were so knocked out that we asked for a day off. John (by wireless) O.K.'d this and then ordered Ang Nima down for a spell and said he was sending Wilf Noyce up to help me with the route above VII and Mike Ward would improve the route between V and VI.

15th May. After 17 hours sleeping I peeped out and saw a trail of chaps leaving V. They arrived about midday – Ed and Wilf with 4 Sherpas. Ed was full of beans and persuaded the Sherpas to carry 25 lbs each on to VII, which they did. A wonderful effort on Ed's part – although he admitted to being tired on the way down. The Sherpas were absolutely flogged.

Wilf stayed and Ang Nima went down. Wilf took a sleeping pill and persuaded me to have one. I swallowed this at 7.30 on the 15th thinking it would give me a good sleep before a very ambitious day on the 16th. I slept like a log and at seven Wilf woke me, and I knelt and started the primus but went to sleep in the kneeling position. All night the wind had been gusty and very strong but I had been oblivious. Then Wilf began to shout and shake me but I was drugged and rolled over and slept until 9 a.m. Through the stupor I could hear Wilf moaning and despairing – beating and shaking me – but I drifted on. Then he slapped and pounded me and I jerked into doing things, got out, swayed on the platform, roped up, and with all our lilos, sleeping bags and things we staggered off. In 2½ hours I was 400 ft above VI and Wilf was worried that I'd die. I looked and wobbled so drunkenly. He suggested lunch and we sat on the slope and opened sardines. I ate one and my head dropped and I was asleep, sliding down the face. Wilf hauled the rope and I could hear him say, "Oh, God what will I do? What will I do? Oh, what has happened!" I mumbled and dribbled and managed to say I was drugged by the sleeping pill and I'd have to go back to VI.

I felt absolutely bloody and so weak, and without any will power. Wilf led me to VI – where I fell and flopped down the slopes and fell into the tent and snored off. He took off rope, crampons and boots, and I was doped until evening. I woke then for two hours but felt awful, and heard Wilf giving a despairing account to Base and asking the doctors what to do – reply – "He'll probably sleep it off by morning". I felt terrible that night and slept log-like and awoke normally and fresh on 17th May. Thank God – never again will they persuade me!

17th May. We established two tents on the site of Swiss VII and in the afternoon Wilf and I pushed on to about 25,000 ft and came down to find Mike Ward here with 4 Sherpas.

Ed Hillary helps to keep the Lhotse Face secure, as he leads a team of Sherpas up to Camp VII.

The view from high on the Lhotse Face, looking back down into the Western Cwm.

From Camp VI, with Sherpa Ang Nima as his companion, George Lowe cut a route up the Lhotse Face.

The Sherpas went down with Wilf and Mike stayed to relieve Wilf and I decided to keep Da Tenzing here as Mike looked knocked by the height.

Everything looked fine for a push today to fix a rope on the last traverse below the South Col and so complete the terrific Lhotse Face job. About 9 p.m. it began to blow and this is the real Everest wind. The tents cracked and rocked and this morning we left at 10 a.m. in a 100 mph gale to try the traverse. We soon iced up and Mike's hands went numb. We ploughed on – I took some movie of the others in the wind until the camera seized. We finally stopped at 25,600 ft with the traverse 300 ft above – but quite out of the question. We came down in terrible conditions and ever since the two tents have been taking a terrific pasting. Now it is dark – I must sleep, hoping the wind will die and tomorrow we'll fix the final ropes, for the South Col carry on the 20th.

Bye, George.

Advanced Base
22nd May 1953

Dear Folks,

The big push is underway. The excitement here is terrific. Everyone is writing furiously now and trying not to be too excited. Right now we look up at the Lhotse Face and see 17 people like ants crawling across the traverse to the South Col. They are about 26,000 ft now! Think what a triumph this is. Today we establish South Col with our main strength down here ready to put in the tremendous final punch. Seventeen people with 30 lb loads, already as high as Annapurna, the highest ever climbed. And down here are two assault teams with oxygen – with support parties on oxygen and 7 super-fit Sherpas (with oxygen) all ready to set off this afternoon and tomorrow for the final crack.

The situation has been balancing like a battle hourly since we came down the day before yesterday. Yesterday afternoon was terrific. The whole thing was in the balance. John looked haggard and drawn. Tom Bourdillon was despairing on the oxygen bottles – none of the first lift would leave Camp VII. Notes were flying, the wireless between here and VII was phut – but the one tremendous thrill was seeing a reccy party hit the South Col – but let's go back.

On 20th – Wilf Noyce and Analu have just returned from South Col with news – and the events mount hourly. How can I get this all down! By a mistake I wasn't with Wilf on his run to South Col and I'm as envious as hell.

On 20th May Mike Ward, Da Tenzing and I left VII at 9.30 a.m. to make an attempt to reach the final traverse before the South Col and so have the route fixed for the Sherpas who were to carry on 21st. On 20th the wind was bad and the cold very formidable. We set out but turned down after only ¾ of an hour. We had all deteriorated considerably and my feet were slightly bitten, Michael's left hand also and Da Tenzing was quite without sting. It was a terrific disappointment to me as it ended my activity on the mountain and I did so hope to reach the South Col. I had been over 25,000 feet on 3 days out of 4 and still felt fitter than the other two. The wireless had failed and we could not get Advanced Base (Camp IV) and John was in a terrific stew. He sent Wilf up on the 20th with a message and an oxygen set for me – with the intention the he (Wilf) and I make an oxygen bid for South Col on 21st and try and persuade the 7 Sherpas to follow.

However our last orders were to come down on 20th – at all costs – and make way for the S. Col lift under Wilf. At midday we went down and met Wilf halfway between VI and VII. Our first news was that we hadn't covered the route to the traverse and it was still in doubt – a disturbing thing for Wilf. Second we said that VII was right out of fuel and was he carrying supplies. He wasn't and for the first time we saw Wilf in a flap. The carry had been going badly and Wilf was quite rattled. We straightened out the fuel problem and took off two of his Sherpas to collect fuel from VI. Here Wilf forgot to tell me about the oxygen attempt and I came down to IV.

We were rather surprised to find John very disappointed at our not reaching the traverse – but it was understandable as he had set such store by our efforts and I had been very cocky. Last night there was a drawn, despondent air in the camp. The 'face' lift was demoralised, the traverse unreached, Wilf's Sherpas had been going badly to VII. The wireless did not connect and John was distraught. I had a bad night as the general feeling, although unsaid, was that I had failed somewhat.

21st dawned fine, and everyone glued eyes on VII. 8 a.m. no sign of shifting – 8.30 a.m., 9 o'clock, 9.15 a.m. John was desperate. Why doesn't Wilf start! I'm sure his Sherpas have failed! Hell, the weather is right, we must get away. 9.30 a.m., no signs of life in Camp VII. 9.45 a.m. and two figures leave VII and start down! Despair and conjecture! What's happened. 10 a.m., two figures leave VII and start up – very slowly. Nothing else. We guessed the two "ups" as Wilf and Analu going up to the traverse to fix ropes and fix the route we had missed.

John decided to despatch Ed and Tenzing to VII on oxygen – a few hours previously Charles Wylie had left with the second seven of the Sherpa lift. John, having guessed that the Sherpas had jibbed, sent Tenzing with Ed to add a solid spur. This was a bold move as Ed and Tenzing were his summit hopes, intended to leave fresh in a day or so. Oxygen could be ill spared but they set off at midday on 21st when no Sherpas left VII.

Midday Wilf and Analu, both on oxygen, were steaming up at a terrific speed (1,000 ft an hour). They reached the Lhotse Face traverse and then headed up the long snow slope for the place above the S. Col where the route leads – 26,400 ft.

A note arrived from Wilf (the two men coming down were Sherpas who jibbed at going up and were sent down with a note) to say that several oxygen bottles were leaking and that the Sherpas at VII refused, in a body, to push up – saying that they were all sick. John tore his hair and retired to his tent, Charles Evans, his chief lieutenant, went to console, Tom Bourdillon began pacing around and shouting over the wireless – "Camp IV calling Camp VII – Report my signals – This is urgent – Over! Repeat, repeat, repeat!" Tom is oxygen officer and wanted to try and save the oxygen. For three hours or so the place was like a battle control room and the battle was going badly – except that Wilf and Analu were forging up and at 2.30 p.m. crossed 26,400 ft and went out of sight to the Col and there was a mental cheer here in Advanced Base. What a thrill it was to see the first party hit the Col.

John was mad keen then that the radio contact with VII be established. At 5 p.m., our usual time, the calls were urgent and strained and <u>no</u> contact was made. We didn't know the Sherpa morale position, the oxygen bottles were reported leaking. The summit parties were due to leave within 24 hours and this would be useless and wasteful of oxygen and energy if the S. Col lift did not go. The S. Col lift was so tight that if only one man failed to lift his 30 lbs the assault could not launch on time. The weather is now as good as it will ever be. Poor John showed the strain far more than anybody.

Bed on 21st but no sleep. 5.30 had seen Wilf and Analu descend from S. Col leaving behind a wonderful trail of helpful steps. All night everybody tossed and turned. Late evening a mail-runner arrived and included a note from James Morris (The Times Special Correspondent at Base) to say that five journalists are camped at Base all waiting with men to race to the nearest wireless base to report the news of the attempt. This is quite fantastic – the first time it's ever happened here. All radio walkie-talkie is now in code in case they pick up our messages direct. The tension down there is terrific.

The night grew gusty – the stars were spot-light bright and a wind moaned and roared over S. Col like a sea-tide. The noise is quite a usual sound now – but this time it had a special meaning. 40° of frost was recorded here.

The 22nd dawned clear and the wind suddenly dropped about 7.30 a.m., although odd wisps could be seen licking Lhotse – a gentle zephyr of 40 or 50 m.p.h. or so!

At 8 a.m. a cry went up from here – "They're on the way – seventeen of them!" There was a rush for glasses and even with the naked eye we could see the great lift across the great crevasses above VII and trailing like a tiny centipede along the slopes of the upper Lhotse Face. The best of glasses made out Ed and Tenzing punching out a track in the snow, aided by precious assault set oxygen. The feeling of good cheer and excitement was great here when we counted that <u>every</u> Sherpa was on the way and the train pushed up and up without pause – 25,000 – 25,600 – up the roped crack – the right hook and then out of the Lhotse Face icefall to the huge couloir – up – up – up – midday, nearly 26,000 and still going, but slowly now. What a triumph! 17 people to 26,000 feet, the weather practically perfect. Spirits rose, the assault team of Charles Evans and Tom Bourdillon and John (in support) checked their gear and prepared to leave for V. About 1.30 one tiny figure stayed on the slope and the rest went on – someone we think has doubled his load (probably Ed or Tenzing). Charles Wylie is there with them too and at 3 p.m. they have all disappeared out of sight, towards the Col.

Then midday 22nd, Wilf and Analu arrive at IV looking fresh – everyone greets them after their great effort. Questions fly, – oxygen O.K.? – Stores at VII? Sherpa lift? South Col stores?

There's enough S. Col stores for the first assault but not enough for the second and main. I've got a job – to get volunteer Sherpas and lift oxygen to S. Col. I'm very excited at this now. It's just been decided.

4 p.m., 22nd. Charles Evans and Tom Bourdillon with the most ultra-futuristic closed-circuit apparatus, plus their own personal gear (lilo, sleeping bags, crampons and what-have-you – over 50 lbs altogether) with John Hunt and two special Sherpas (Ang Temba and Balu) on open circuit, set off for V to spend the night, then VII tomorrow. South Col, 24th and summit attempt 25th. This was quite a moment.

Now on morning of 24th, Ed and Tenzing – second summit team supported by Gregory and three super Sherpas to place Ridge Camp (28,000?) with me and three Sherpas to lift oxygen to S. Col are due to leave – and so this tangled account had better end for now.

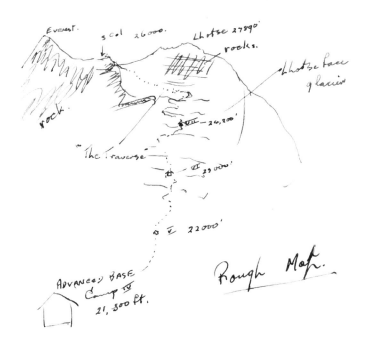

CHAPTER FOUR

Base Camp
1st June 1953

Dear Betty,

In a day or so the world will know of our success. At present don't imagine our band of thirteen rolling and rollicking in an ecstasy brought on by victory. If you were at Base Camp now you would see nine Sahibs and about fifteen Sherpas lying listlessly around the tents with bloodshot and glazed eyes, thin, dirty and bewildered. Ed now is sleeping as he has done for hours and hours; Charles is just smoking and tired; the talk is very desultory and dull; everyone is quite played out. Five of the other lads will be descending tomorrow from Camp III and they too will come in stiff legged and flogged after the last two weeks.

Two days ago we were on the South Col urging ourselves to the limit – and now like pricked balloons all our reserves have

On 25 May the second assault party, Ed and Tenzing, left Camp IV. Here Tenzing prepares the flags that he would later unfurl on the summit.

gone. Yesterday, we came down to Base Camp. Ed, Charles Evans and I were together on one rope and it took hours. I have never been so tired, nor had Ed. Now, if you could see us, you would see the most beaten, played-out, lustreless team of climbers that it is possible to imagine.

I last wrote on 22nd May and since then I have been very high, and the summit has been reached. You will know something of the event from the newspapers but here is as far as I can recall it, the day to day happenings from 22nd.

When the great lift reached the South Col on 22nd John Hunt decided to launch the Assault Plan and accordingly the closed circuit boys went into action. Tom Bourdillon and Charles Evans set off on the afternoon of 22nd with all their bedding tied around their closed circuit apparatus, with spare soda-lime canisters and spanners poking out – in all some 50 lbs. John Hunt went with them on open circuit as support and possible emergency. Two Sherpas also went (Da Namgyl and Balu, two specially chosen Sherpas) to carry a tent and oxygen above the South Col as a possible emergency ration and shelter in the case of a late descent by Tom and Charles. In the event of this tent and oxygen not being used it was to be added to by the second assault party (Ed and Tenzing) backed by Gregory and three special Sherpas.

It was at this stage that I came into the story. The original plan did not include me but I was very keen to get to South Col. Because of Ed and Tenzing's trip to South Col with the Sherpa lift, and their consequent tiredness, they decided to wait a day longer than the original plan. Then it was discovered, mostly by my propaganda, that a little more oxygen and food would be advisable. Accordingly, I was commissioned to escort five Sherpas to South Col along with

Gregory and his three special Ridge Camp boys to back up Ed and Tenzing. I spent all 23rd May frantically trying to fix a leak in the oxygen set I was to use. Finally by cutting and binding one of the rubber feed pipes I stopped the hiss. Tom, Charles and John climbed to Camp VII on 23rd.

24th May. Tom, Charles and John with their two Sherpas crept above Camp VII and worked slowly to South Col. We watched them through glasses, they were slow, seven hours, and arrived late and very tired. On 24th we packed up and Greg and I with our Sherpas left for Camp V, where we spent the night (a cold night, our thermometer read -27° Centigrade at 5 a.m.).

25th May. Tom and Charles were timed to make an attempt on the South Peak and summit if possible using closed circuit. Due to the weather (wind) and their tired condition from previous day they stayed on South Col. Greg and I left for VI using oxygen (2 litres per minute). We made good time, and at VI changed to 4 litres and we headed up on the Lhotse Face for VII. You will remember that the climb from V to VII is up the difficult Lhotse Face on which nearly 1,000 ft of rope is fixed. Above VI I began to falter. I began to pant and weaken although Greg was making a slow pace. I began to worry and think I was failing – but it turned out to be a defect in my oxygen set which was cutting right out and the mask was stopping even the outside air getting in. The trip to VII, for me, was hell and I collapsed on the snow at VII and took a couple of hours to recover. At VII I was able to trace the trouble and the set behaved beautifully the next day. Ed and Tenzing came right through to VII from IV that day and arrived fresh and fit.

Although Everest was blowing a cloud plume on these days the weather was very settled and the weather report (from

Indian radio) gave us: "Warm temperatures, winds 15-20 knots and settled weather. Monsoon still only in the Andaman Sea". Camp VII (24,000 ft approximately) was calm that night (Temp -28° Centigrade).

26th May. We left VII at 8.45 a.m. and had wonderful conditions for our climb to South Col. I filmed much of the climb and felt really wonderful. The climb starts near the top of the Lhotse Face glacier and for perhaps a thousand feet is a steady crampon climb up crevassed slopes and then swings left to traverse above rock bands and goes diagonally and up the great snow slopes towards the Col. The South Col is not reached direct. The rock buttress of 'Eperon de Genevois' stops this and our route connected with the very top of the Eperon over which we climbed and dropped several hundred feet into the South Col (25,850 ft).

About 1 p.m. on 26th we began traversing rock and snow at the top of the Eperon. The South Peak of Everest was in view (the South Peak is a beautiful snow peak and sweeps up looking incredibly steep) and on the final slope I saw two dots, like flies on a wall, about two hundred feet below the cornice of the top. We went mad with excitement as we watched Tom and Charles go steadily up and over the South Summit (28,720 ft) and, we thought, off for the main summit. They were higher than anyone ever before and apparently going at a very fast rate. They had climbed from the South Col that morning and reached the South Summit in 5½ hours. John, too, had set out with Da Namgyl (both on open circuit) ahead of Tom and Charles to carry Ridge Camp, but with the closed circuit they easily overtook him and far outclassed the open circuit at the highest altitudes. Balu, the other Sherpa, had failed – in fact he refused to go above the South Col.

Greg and I were so excited at seeing Tom and Charles that we ran down into the Col Camp to shout the news to Ed and Tenzing. Ed came out of the Dome tent with a great whoop and then dived back again. Tenzing, we were hurt to find, lost his smile and did not share our enthusiasm. The idea of team effort had not been revealed to him and the idea that anybody but Tenzing should reach the summit was not pleasurable to him.

Ed's disappearance into the dome I thought strange and I pushed my way in to find John lying quite exhausted with Ed plying drinks and oxygen. Ed and Tenzing had arrived on the Col before us and Ed saw John returning with Da Namgyl from his ridge carry. John and Da N. had carried to 27,350 ft and were returning completely done in. John was staggering and crumpling and staggering on again, when Ed rushed off to help him. Ed assisted him on his shoulder and slapped his oxygen mask on him for a good half hour (John's oxygen had run out at 27,350 and he came down without). Da Namgyl's hands were frostbitten and he was very tired. I went in to see John and he said amongst other things: "Do you know, the most awful thing about being completely shagged?" – "You piddle your pants and can do nothing about it!"

John certainly earned our admiration – he's got tremendous guts. This day he pushed himself to the absolute limit – but this was typical of him all through.

There were three tents on South Col; a Pyramid, a Dome and a Meade. They respectively housed four, two and two. The Pyramid had previously been used by Sherpas and was in a disgraceful condition. The floor was in shreds and parting at the stitching at the seams. The windward side had a four-inch tear which later caused great inconvenience by admitting drifting snow and cold wind. The rope guys were far too light and in the tremendous and ceaseless buffeting on the Col they were fraying and broken when we arrived. Ed and I went out in the afternoon into a freezing roaring wind and began to repair the tent. We found a pile of strong Swiss line and began replacing all the guys and placing rocks around the worst tears in the floor to protect it from the plucking of the wind.

During this time, the S. Summit became enveloped in cloud and we began to worry about Tom and Charles. We knew, as they knew, that if their closed circuit sets failed in any way (and they had many gadgets, valves, tubes and canisters susceptible to error) they would not come back. Tom was an exceedingly determined thruster and we felt his enthusiasm would overcome good sense – but Ed remarked "Charles is pretty sensible – I think he'll balance Tom".

About this time the three Sherpas who had been chosen to carry with Greg to the Ridge Camp arrived on the Col from Camp VII. They had set out with us and gone slowly and badly. This was disturbing as we had placed high hopes on them. They were Amg Temba, Pemba and Ang Nima. Ang Temba we thought the best, and were amazed to find that when he dumped his load (30 lbs) outside the tent he keeled over and for ten minutes was out cold. Pemba was very tired while Ang Nima was quite fresh and unaffected by the altitude.

John by this time had recovered and was fretting about Tom and Charles. He kept peering up the ridge looking for their return. The afternoon passed and we all became more and more worried. As we fixed the last ropes I saw some moving dots at the head of the couloir, by which they had reached the ridge. I watched until, in the shifting mist, I was certain and shouted the news. Our relief was tremendous.

Their descent of the couloir was frightening to watch. Dog-tired, they started down one at a time, each anchoring the other and each falling off as they tried to kick downhill. They slid and fell their rope lengths, each just managing to hold the other. As Tom said, "We yo-yo'd our way down – it was quite fun!"

Ed and I went out to meet them, and I filmed their arrival. They were still wearing and using their closed circuit and apart from the masks which covered nose, mouth and chin they were covered in icicles. Ice driblets from the mask outlet had stuck to their windproofs and they were panting and labouring just to move along the flat.

They had not gone far beyond the South Summit – a few yards only – their soda lime canisters did not leave them with enough time in hand to risk going on. The summit ridge seemed long (Tom judged 2 or 3 hours and Charles thought 4 or more), it was corniced and had a difficult vertical rock step in it. Tom took 18 photographs and they turned down. Just below the South Summit they jettisoned two oxygen bottles having enough left to get to South Col. These bottles were a vital help in getting Ed and Tenzing to the top two days later.

That night Ed, Tenzing, Greg and I slept in the pyramid; John, Tom and Charles squashed into the two-man Meade, while Ang Temba, Pemba and Ang Nima passed the night in the even smaller Dome. That night for everyone was pure misery. The wind slammed over the Col and worried the tents, whining, roaring and snapping incessantly. It became the curse of the Col, sapping our tempers and eating indelibly into our memories. We will never forget the South Col. We all spent there the most miserable days and nights of our lives.

The temperature dropped until we were all cold even though fully dressed (we wore our high altitude boots in the sleeping bags to stop them freezing) with full down clothing and our warm sleeping bags. I have never been so miserable with freezing feet (they were lightly frost-bitten – getting better now), cold knees and back which was rammed hard against the windward side of the tent. My pillow was a kit bag full of frozen snow – hard, cold and unsatisfactory. What a night! But it was only the first of four which grew increasingly worse.

At 4.30 a.m. we began to prepare breakfast in the hope of an early start in carrying Ridge Camp. Our appetites were good – we had carried up some 'luxury food' and ate the lot at breakfast. I remember the menu – 'vita-wheat' biscuits with honey; sardines on biscuit ('vita-wheat'); two tins of pineapple (between 4); slices of saucisson (salami or raw bacon sausage), biscuits and honey and lastly a tin of Australian pears. We ate and spread honey with gloves on and you can imagine what a messy business it was.

Our hopes of starting faded when at 8 a.m. the wind velocity had increased to over 70 or 80 m.p.h. and never looked like decreasing. All day, 27th May, it blew and put the chances of climbing on a ridge out of the question.

Supplies on the Col were limited and Charles and Tom had to go down. Ang Temba was so sick that he too was to go down. John, too, although he felt as leader he should stay to see and support the main assault, decided to go down and leave me to join the Ridge carry. With Ang Temba out of the carry, someone had to replace him, and I was fit. So again, although not supposed in the plan to stay on South Col, I was now in the ridge party.

Ang Temba, Tom, Charles and John left in the howling wind. Their climb to the top of the Eperon (500 ft) took nearly two hours. Ed and I assisted them – they were dreadfully weak but once over the Eperon they were out of the worst wind and going downhill. Their journey to VII was an epic and there they were received by Wilfrid Noyce and Mike Ward. On 28th they limped to Advanced Base, to good food, attention and rest.

For the remainder of 27th May we sat out the wind and dreaded the coming of night. The night was a repetition of the previous one and in the morning we were stiff, bad-tempered, ill-fed with very frayed morale. The wind mercifully eased and we stiffly prepared to go. Three hours it took to make a few simple preparations. Then an apparently crippling blow fell. Pemba suddenly spewed over the tent floor and began to groan and said he couldn't go. That left one Sherpa, Ang Nima, and we needed three. That hour the expedition hopes recorded their lowest reading!

After a discussion we agreed to try and lift the two extra Sherpa loads between us. The weights were about 45 lbs each which seemed Herculean when a good load <u>at this altitude</u> was considered to be 15 lbs.

Greg, Ang Nima and I got away at 8.45 a.m. Ed and Tenzing decided to delay at least an hour to save their strength and oxygen while we cut steps up the couloir. We were heavily clothed and with the loads we stomped along like robots. We made a very slow steady pace which we managed to hold without stopping and began to make height. The wind dropped to a comparative

Ed Hillary at 27,200 ft on the South-East Ridge, the day before his successful ascent.

breeze and we slugged up into the couloir and I began cutting steps. Cutting steps at 27,000 is an experience – a study in 'go slow'. It took three hours to get up to the ridge (27,200 ft) where we saw the wreckage of the Swiss top camp (one tent) with not a vestige of the cloth on the aluminium bones. Here we dropped our loads and enjoyed the tremendous view. Lhotse and Makalu were wonderful, Kangchenjunga jutted out above the clouds. Below was the Kangshung and Kharta glaciers with wonderful views of brown Tibet beyond.

Oddly enough I enjoyed and remembered the couloir climb and the view as if it were at sea-level. I had read that altitude robbed both these. With me it was not so. Here Ed and Tenzing caught up with us. Greg was going exceedingly well, Ang Nima the same and we urged him on by saying that if he went a bit higher he would have carried and gone higher than any Sherpa in the world. He was very ambitious and carried magnificently. About 150 ft above here we reached John's highest point and found the rolled tent, food, an R.A.F. oxygen cylinder and other oddments and these we had to add to our loads. Ed took the tent, Greg the R.A.F. cylinder and I took food oddments and some of Greg's load and we left there with Ed carrying 63 lbs; Greg 50 lbs; self 50 lbs; Ang Nima 45 lbs and Tenzing 43 lbs.

From here the ridge is moderately steep – odd broken rock and towers followed by snow ridge. I led and the snow was bloody – knee deep and loose. From then on the upward progress was grim-dead-brained toil. I don't really know how we endured the weight. We pushed up to where we thought a flat spot would be and found it quite untenable. We pushed on again – and again the same thing – and so on. About 2.30

p.m. we stopped below a snow shoulder and found a tiny ledge where we dumped our loads. Ed and Tenzing began clearing a site which was too small for the tent. Snow flurries were beginning and although very tired we set off within two minutes of arrival after cheery banter to and from Ed on the chances for the morrow. The height of Camp IX – Ridge Camp – has been estimated at 27,900 ft.

Our return was slow and tough. Greg had cracked up, Ang Nima was very tired and I had to recut steps all the way down the couloir. From the couloir Greg was collapsing every 50 yards and gasping with exhaustion. I was tired – dreadfully tired – but quite able to keep going without pause, and funnily enough with sufficient mentality to appreciate the glorious evening colours over Kangchenjunga and Makalu. I photographed them. Near the tents I unroped and pushed on. Pemba had made a hot drink and I tossed this down, grabbed the movie camera, staggered out and sitting against a rock, filmed the arrival of Greg and Ang Nima which I hope shows something of the state of really flogged men. We drank hot lemon and tea and crawled into our bags – but not to sleep. The night, the wind and the cold came and we passed another bloody night.

Bloodiest for Greg because he spent an agonising 1½ hours groaning and straining in the darkness of our tent trying to get his bowels to function. Outside on the Col was so miserable, and the desire caught him soon after dozing off. He was so constipated and so exhausted that he couldn't manage his task and for an hour and a half he knelt groaning and straining over an old tin at my feet. I was too tired to care and just lay careless of his deep trouble. He remembers it as his most terrible experience.

The 29th May finally dawned. On the Col it was windy – it was always windy. The sun hit the top of the tent about 5 a.m. It crept down the walls releasing the frost of condensed breath in a shower over us – as usual. Greg had decided to go down as he was too weak to be of use to any returning summit party. Ang Nima and Pemba went down too and left me alone on the Col to receive Ed and Tenzing. At 8 o'clock we saw Ed and T. on the way up the final slopes of the South Summit – going slowly but steadily. At 9 a.m. they disappeared over the S. Summit and somehow then I felt that they would reach the summit. I boiled soup and lemonade and filled the two thermos flasks we had. I prepared oxygen bottles with all connections and masks ready for instant use and set bedding ready as if to receive casualties.

Outside I prepared the spare oxygen frame with the two emergency cylinders which I intended to carry up and meet them to assist their descent.

At 1 p.m. they appeared again on S. Summit and began the descent of the steep loose snow slope. I was wildly excited and leapt into action. I packed the thermos flasks, slung the movie camera in (4 lbs) – put on crampons, gloves – vaselined my nose, face and lips against the wind, tied a scarf round my face for extra protection (I was severely wind-burnt and the skin was frost-affected from the other days and very sore); got into the oxygen carrying frame with two bottles and set off to meet the boys. About 400 yards from camp I began to feel groggy – I was carrying too much, had started too excited and too fast. After the previous day's effort I was not as good as I thought. I looked up and saw Ed and T. were coming down quite fast and steadily and were so far away that I could be of no immediate help so I tottered back to the tent. There I watched them from the tent door. They stopped at Camp IX at 2 p.m. and didn't leave there until 3 p.m. (they had a boil-up of lemonade and collected their sleeping bags) and came down the ridge and then the couloir going absolutely steadily.

Just before 4 p.m. I set out again to meet them, and as I left the tents Wilf Noyce arrived with Pasang Phutar. He had been sent up by John as a useful support to receive and help the summit party in case they were exhausted. It was good to see them and they began to prepare hot drinks as I left.

I dragged up again and met Ed and T. at the foot of the couloir – perhaps 500 ft above the Col. They were moving fairly rapidly – the only tiredness showed in their slightly stiff-legged walking as they cramponned the last bit of the couloir. I crouched, back against the wind and poured out the thermos contents as they came up. Ed unclipped his mask and grinned a tired greeting, sat on the ice and said in his matter of fact way, "Well, we knocked the bastard off!"

It was not quite matter-of-fact – he was slightly incredulous of what he had done. Although I had a feeling they had been successful, the statement roused in me a terrific surge of emotion and relief. Tenzing, though tired, was all smiles and I congratulated them both enthusiastically and Ed's remark was "It was a wonderful climb – but if you'd have been there you'd have done the same."

We walked down to the tents talking ninety to the dozen about the climb. Their return was the most normal of any party on the Col. They walked up to the tents, swung off their oxygen sets, unroped and crawled into the tents, chatting all the time of the climb. We all drank huge quantities of coffee and lemonade and talked until late that night. Wilf, Ed and I squeezed ourselves into the Meade while T. and Pasang Phutar slept in the Dome.

Ed will – I hope – write fully of the climb, but here are a few details. The day went according to plan – they sat the night out in Camp IX (the platform was too small to lie on), they dozed and brewed drinks and left at 6.30 a.m. on 3 litres of oxygen per minute. 9 a.m. South Summit (the last part a very steep climb up bad snow). The summit ridge was corniced and steep and Ed led for 2½ hours cutting steps all the way. He, himself, said he felt good all the way, and was able to cut and move steadily without pause. A rock step – vertical 40 ft – was climbed by a chimney in which he worked back and knee and the last part was tantalising because of crest after crest without the top. Finally at 11.30 they came to 'the perfect summit' – a sharp snow cone on which they looked down on everything. "Tenzing was so excited that he embraced me", said Ed, "It's the perfect summit, every main ridge comes up to it and you can look down each one. I took a photograph looking down every ridge and one of Tenzing on top waving the flags that he had carried up. I think they were the United Nations, Union Jack, Indian and French flags, but I'm not sure."

They took off their oxygen sets and walked around, Ed photographing and Tenzing pointing out Thyangboche monastery in Nepal and Shekar Dzong away in Tibet. There was a steady breeze but otherwise a perfect and clear day. Ed collected a pocket full of stones (8 or 9) from the top and brought them down – he gave me the first and it's quite a treasure. He left there a crucifix that a devout R.C. had given to John Hunt for the purpose. Tenzing left a small offering of food – a Buddhist custom.

Then, with worries about oxygen supply, they hurried down after only a ¼ hour on top. Late that night talk dwindled on. Our fourth night on the South Col was another bloody, windy, cold night.

30th May we left the Col at 10 a.m. abandoning the tents to be snapped at and worried by the mad wind until like the Swiss camp they were just bare frames and torn fabric. We climbed over the Eperon, took a last look at the sweep of the South Summit and pounded down and down the 4,000 ft of traverse and the fixed ropes and crevasses of the Lhotse Face.

At VII Charles Wylie was there to receive us with tea and whoops of joy. We went straight on, passed VI and V, and in the afternoon met Tom Stobart near V. He was filming and as I approached him, I gave the 'thumbs-up' sign and he went mad. He told us John and everyone were waiting at IV (Advanced Base) and were nearly mad with anxiety and conjecture and had asked him to wave a windproof if we had got up. Here we entered a conspiracy and decided to make no sign, walk up to Camp IV and surprise them with the news. Tom was keen because he wanted to film the ensuing scene.

We pushed on towards IV and when a quarter mile away and in view of the tents John and nearly everybody began to come up to meet us to see what the news was. We plodded towards them, excited as hell, but not making any sign. John, we could see, had decided we had failed. His shoulders were slumped and he walked wearily and slowly, thinking dismal thoughts. The others were hesitant as to whether to make the effort to meet us and hear the worst. Tom had his movie and was with us saying, "Not yet! Wait a bit, get closer." Then, when John was perhaps 100 yards away I shoved up my thumb and waved the victory news.

John stopped and gaped, Mike Westmacott began to run and the others did varying things from cheering to crying. John cried. He ran forward, hugged Ed and Tenzing with tears running down his face. He had put so much work and worry into his efforts that the tension broke him. Tom filmed some rather un-English scenes of emotion. Even later, John was so overcome that he retired to his tent so stirred that he couldn't talk and Mike, the doctor, gave him sedatives and put him onto oxygen. What a thrill it was for everybody – all talking in the tent. The expedition, after all the trials and work and hope was now a success. The top was reached and everyone was safe and well. We were so glad that a British party had reached the 'third pole' after over 30 years of trying. That night we toasted the old Everesters, John, the Sherpas, Eric Shipton and talked far into the night.

31st May. The first of us moved to Base Camp while the Sherpas began to lift all that was required down to Base ready for the long march home.

From that day on we went flat. Charles Evans, Ed and I came down on one rope and dreadful tiredness caught us as it did everyone after the tremendous efforts of getting up. The icefall descent was difficult and dangerous and it was nearly dark when we reached Base Camp where for two days we never left our sleeping bags. There, with bloodshot eyes and wasted bodies, we heard the Coronation broadcasts on the radio and then the news of our success on the radio which seemed to buck us up. On Coronation night we toasted the Queen and the Duke with a noggin of rum. The quantity was hardly an egg-cup full each, but such was our depleted state that nearly everyone was made quite drunk and garralous and we passed the evening in singing and merriment.

Hunt, Hillary, Tenzing, Ang Nima, Gregory and Lowe on 30 May at Camp IV, the day after the summit of Everest had been reached.

CHAPTER FIVE

Base Camp
2nd June 1953

Dear Betty, Mum, Dad and All,

This will be short as the mail-runner is off tomorrow with all the important despatches and cables.

Probably at this hour or half day you will hear by radio of our success. Ed and Tenzing reached the summit at 11.30 last Friday 29th May. I was watching them from S. Col and went up to meet them on their descent to camp. It was quite a terrific moment. N.Z. was well to the front – as well as the Lhotse Face work I got onto S. Col where I spent 4 nights and 5 days and carried a 50 lb load to Camp IX at 27,900 ft.

I hope to tell you in detail of the past ten days as we march out to Katmandu. We reached Base on 31st May and arrived absolutely played out and today – after two days of sleeping and eating we are just perking up.

Today is a great day – we are all around the wireless listening to the Coronation service. The crown is just being placed and there is quite a hush amongst the boys. The Duke of Edinburgh is the patron of this expedition and has sent telegrams of goodwill and we are excited by the fact that today he will hear the news of our success.

You can't imagine how profound this success of ours is going to be. We haven't realised it properly yet. It hasn't come without effort and trying.

Today a cable from Holyoake (acting Prime M.) arrived and we thought it rather a thrill. Thanks to all the family for the very comforting and encouraging cable you sent me – I received it the day I came down when dog-tired but with the knowledge that the trials were over. It was a nice thought.

The cable from Holyoake: "N.Z. is watching the courage and determination of the Everest expedition with the closest interest and deep admiration. Already your efforts have served to raise still further the high prestige which the 1951 Himalayan expedition gave to N.Z. mountaineers and to yourself. I wish you and your companions every success in your second attempt on the peak. Acting Prime Minister."

The day after tomorrow we are setting out for the long trek back to Katmandu. We expect to arrive there about 17th June and expect to be there five or seven days.

Ed, Tenzing and John (I think) will be flying to England and John has cabled the Himalayan Committee asking if they will authorise the flying to England of the rest of the party. I would like a flip by Comet – which is the service from Delhi (17 hours to London!) But somehow I don't think the Committee will come over with the money for us 'lesser mortals'.

In the mess tent at Base Camp on 2 June, the team heard news of their Everest success over the wireless. Band, Hillary, Evans and Ward are pictured here.

If we fly I'll be in England by the end of June – if we sail we'll be there about the beginning of August.

I'm looking forward to the trip and visit to England – all the English boys are full of invitations and promise both of us a wonderful time. I'm glad that Ed is going even if it is only for a few weeks. Ed insists that he get home in September for the start of the season. But as yet all these are tentative plans that might not come off.

I have been very thrilled on receiving letters from the brothers and sisters (Chris and Mabel were the latest) all expressing interest in my doings and as I have said especially for the cable of goodwill before the big effort. Ed, too thanks you for your good wishes.

As you will have guessed, Ed was the dominant member of the expedition and his final effort was right in keeping with what he had been doing all along. Tenzing was quite pale in comparison. I am not discrediting Tenzing's wonderful endurance – but he was very second to Ed. It would be a pity if anyone thought Tenzing led Ed up. They were a superb team together.

More anon during the walk out. Love to all the brothers, sisters and families, to the Watts', and to all the people who have followed our doings with such close interest, my kindest regards.

Cheers, George.

On 2nd June we moved down to Loje, the first green grass, stream and flowers off the Khumbu glacier. It rained – the first rain we had experienced in two months. We had been too high for rain before. The evening was perfect and someone suggested we shoot off the mortar bombs in honour of the Queen. We did this to the astonishment of the Sherpas.

By now we were recovering our strength and morale and we sang around a roaring brush fire. The Sherpas caught our spirit and the 'high altitude' boys began a Sherpa dance which grew and grew until they were all in it around the lanterns singing and stamping their traditional dances.

The Sherpa dance is rather like a Russian cossack dance and is accompanied by a chant that is rather English Churchish. I wish we had a tape recorder here – it was a most memorable night.

The 3rd June dawned gloriously, with birds singing around the camp. A new warmth soaked into us. Most of the boys whistled or sang as they packed their gear. They wandered off in twos and threes gassing about rock climbing in Wales or the glory of the view. We were beginning to respond to the healing effects of low altitude and growing things. All the day we paused to notice birds, berries, violets, azaleas, moss on the stream beds, and young leaf on the first trees.

Charles Evans told us of his silver pig. He had a small silver pig that was sent to Eric Shipton with the story that after the First World War a girl gave it to Somerville as he left on the 1924 Everest show (when Mallory died). Somerville took the pig with him to 28,000 ft on the Tibetan side, took it home to England and gave it back to the little girl. The girl grew and married and gave the silver pig to her son. The little boy sent it to Shipton in 1951 and it accompanied Eric. This year Eric gave it to Charles who took it with him to the South Summit and he gave it to Tenzing on the South Col. Tenzing took it to the top and returned it to Charles – who is now sending it back to the little boy. Lucky boy!

On the March
11th June 1953

The fifth day of the march home. The writing of this when I was dog tired at Base and Loje was a marathon which I could never repeat. Now the trek home is a third done, there are many things to add but I expect I'll forget them before I can write them down. It's nearly dusk and the daily rain discourages attempts to write.

To continue the tale:– From Loje, the place where the Sherpas danced, we walked in one long day to Thyangboche. At the monastery the water-hole had dried up and we went back down the hill to a little village called Mingbo and camped in a field where a tiny creek gave us a supply of water. Mingbo became paradise. The tents sprang up and for three days we dozed, ate, read, talked and were satisfactorily lazy. Nearby were thousands of primulas in bloom which we wandered over to look at. We found a blue poppy and watched the lammergaus (huge eagles) cruising overhead.

Mingbo is a place of some 8 or 10 houses and consists almost exclusively (according to Tenzing) of ex nuns and lamas who have married. Thyangboche, the monastery, is 20 minutes walk up the hill from the nunnery, and it seems that attachments form and become too strong for their celibate vows and the 'fallen ones' take up residence in Mingbo. I don't wonder at some marriages as the women we saw there were exceedingly attractive. The most striking one had a wonderful Tibetan hat with gold brocaded adornments. She was always bringing gifts of milk, dai and food to Tenzing. We teased him about this and he explained that he had discovered her son in Darjeeling – and seeing him going to the bad there, had brought him back to Mingbo when we trekked in during March. For this she was showing gratitude.

The day of our return to Thyangboche the abbot promised to have performed for us the devil dances. In the monastery are a whole series of highly painted devil masks and dress after dress of very ornate and costly silk robes which go with the masks.

Usually the dance ceremonies take all day and with these outfits they dance and depict various incidents, passions and characters which they mime. Several of the dances were done for us, but we failed to get any useful interpretation of what was going on. Tom Stobart and I filmed it in colour, the lighting was bad, but I hope to have something to show you. Tom filmed with one camera from their great open dance quadrangle while I was set up on the balcony that surrounds this and on which the head lama – in full regalia on his throne – sits, with the drums, cymbals and the great long (18 ft) alpine horns and other gadgets that supply music and rhythm. In between dance acts they plied us with Tibetan tea, chapatties and rakshi (rice spirits, which looks and tastes like methylated!)

As the dance was in progress an aeroplane was roaring over Everest and our way. Unidentified – four engined, fast-moving plane similar to one that flew over Everest in April on 8 days in succession. It was back again the following day and each time disappeared flying north over Tibet.

After a day in Mingbo, John, Greg and Tom B. left to make a fast trip through to Katmandu in order to facilitate baggage and travel arrangements and fix many official things. The night before they left was the final night on which we would all be together as an expedition. The spirit was marvellous and we had to agree that this had been a splendid expedition. The team-work had been superb and now after all these months everyone were the best of companions and there had not been a single incident of unfriendliness. They are a great bunch of easy going chaps and we congratulated John on his careful choice.

We, the main party of nine, were delayed a day by the difficulty of raising 100 porters who would carry to Katmandu now that the monsoon had come and the high level routes were to be used.

We left on 7th June and passed through Namche on the way. Many of our high altitude Sherpas had been paid off and were resident there and they met us and insisted we visit their house and be entertained. We pushed on a few hours later very full of chang, potatoes and eggs – sad in a way to bid the boys farewell. Nearly all our Sherpas were drunk and we didn't get far – just far enough to shake the influences of Namche – and made our first camp.

The second day down the Dudh Kosi gorges and climbed to a few houses and camped during a hail storm at Tate. Here, a returning mail-runner met us and we read 'The Times' (only ten days old!), 'The Weekly News' and three letters from home. The reason for the regular mail-service was a blessing brought by the many newspaper men that penetrated here. Every day during the assault they sent off despatches and bribed the runners great sums if they raced their rivals. Consequently for a two week period more than one runner a day left from Everest carrying despatches and they also carried our mail. Now they are returning home and daily for the last four days we've had mail – until today we received 'The Times' only 7 days from London.

Today, too, came a sheaf of congratulatory cables and we are all delighted. The Queen, Philip, Winston Churchill, Swiss Alpine Club, French, British, Canadian and many others, and literally dozens of private ones. I was very pleased that Dad sent the 'Sunnybank' one to John Hunt and congratulated the whole team. John is very keen on the 'whole team' idea and he will receive this with great pleasure. I will have to thank Betty, the Hill Family, the Mayor – a very nice one – Greater Hastings, Jim Rose and many other thoughtful people. Sid Holland sent a very good one to John – Ed of course has received streams. Altogether, we feel rather pleased with ourselves.

Today we crossed a 15,000 ft pass – in the mist – and dropped down and down a long ridge to Ringmo. The last part was along a ridge through bush very like N.Z. There were great straight barrelled trees, ferns and lush undergrowth.

I think a mail-runner is going ahead, so I'll stop. This will cost something! Love to Mum and Dad and all. Thanks for the cuttings and letters and especially the cables. Am well and enjoying the walk out.

Regards to all, George.

Chaubas, On the March
18th June 1953

Dear Betty,

At this moment we are enduring a violent monsoon thunderstorm. The thunder is continuous and the rain torrential. The tent floor is soaking from the running off water and the sport is to write and avoid the drips. I'm sitting like a hen on a pile of gear trying to keep it dry. Da Namgyl is channelling around the tent with an ice axe trying to entice the water away. What fun travelling in the monsoon is! This will bring the leeches out.

The day after tomorrow we'll be in Katmandu – Hooray! Hooray because we'll be away from this daily rain and amongst good food and drink with real beds, baths and things.

This 15 day march home has been made a great joy by the <u>daily</u> mail-runners sent to us from Katmandu. The flood of mail has been fantastic – the cables absolutely in undreamed of numbers from many kind people. The good thing is that everybody seems to have caught on to the team spirit idea and everybody in the party has had a wonderful share of personal and party cables. Ed and John of course head the list with <u>me</u> a close second. Everyone has been very kind to think of us all collectively. Yesterday was the heaviest day yet. Ed with 47 letters and 36 cables (he already has 150) and me with 38 letters and 15 cables (I already had 33). It's terrific what goodwill and pleasure this event has touched off – and we're glad. I hope to acknowledge as many good wishes as I can, but the postage will shock me!

I have received letters and cables from – well here are a <u>few</u> – Greater Hastings, Mayor Jaycees, Junior Chamber of Commerce, Herald Tribune (a very nice one), High School, Wgtn. Teachers Training College plus a letter from principal Jonah, Hillary's Otamauri School, (John Paton), Waiwhare, Chapmans, Luxtons, Thorsbys, Miss Roy, Jim Rose, Alpine Club, Hills, Harry Ayres, Chris, Mabel, Jenny, Poppy, Arch, Geoff Milne, Heretaungas, N.Z. Educational Institute, Dick and Helen Arthur, Doug Ashby, all old girl friends! and Betty and lots more. I must admit it is all rather pleasant getting this flood.

In two days the social round will begin. Five days we have in Katmandu and are booked for more social functions than five! The King is coming out to Badgaon (the road end) to meet us for a civic reception – just as we are – dirty, unshaven and hungry.

Then we fly to Delhi and meet Nehru and all that and fly to England on 1st or 2nd July. What a do! I won't be going to Bombay and will have to get stuff there sent on.

Sir Edmund is well – as are all the boys. We got the knighthood news on 14th as we came over a pass, and Ed wouldn't believe it. Then he nearly passed out when an official note came from Summerhayes, the Ambassador. He was most embarrassed. All the lads are pleased that he and John got it – but it was a bit of a shock to see how wildly enthusiastic England had gone about all this. Ed said "If I see Philip, I'll tell him he's overdoing it a bit. This knighthood business is going too far!" The enthusiasm which has been shown over the success was absolutely unexpected and it wasn't until the knighthood came through that we realised how deeply it had gone.

I'm looking forward to all the official do's and famous meetings – I expect we'll get sick of it, but it will be a worthwhile experience.

Thanks for cuttings and letters. And thanks especially to Mum for the one from her.

Katmandu
22nd June 1953

Back again. This town is a mad-house, all gone crazy about Tenzing. Unfortunately the whole thing is political squabbling and the superiority of the Eastern races and the dirt flying is rather sticky. The arrival in Katmandu was an absolute 'Alice in Wonderland' scene of pantomime – it would take a dozen pages to tell – more anon perhaps. But just imagine us all there in tennis shoes and stinking shirts, bearded, hungry and dying for a bath. Pugh was in a pair of pyjamas, just as he had been during his walk out from Namche. A royal reception at the palace with Tenzing and family, Ed and John and 8 others in a royal coach (to hold four!!) drawn by four wild chestnut horses. T. received the equivalent of knighthood, while John and Ed got the Order of the Ghurkha Right Hand – 1st Class.

Every afternoon and night there were official receptions, cocktail parties, then dinners and all taken much too seriously by us. I'm lucky – I'm looking after the repacking, labelling and sending of baggage and excused these 'dos'.

We are flying to Patna 25th June, where I shall be recording a talk for All India Radio. John and Ed are going to Calcutta. Then we fly to Delhi on 26th and are caught up by John and Ed. There we meet Nehru and dozens of other Indian receptions. On 1st July we fly to London.

Thanks for many things, Betty. The food parcels, the cakes, the photos of Jenny's new boy, the sending of letters (it's O.K. to send these but repeat the note about copyright.)

Yes I shall want my overcoat. The parcel containing the woollen shirts has not come yet and I'll get the Embassy to send them on.

I haven't been able to write any letters since returning and I think my output will be greatly reduced for some time to come. Until I can write to Chris, would you thank her for the letter and the parcel of tongues – it is very kind of her.

Thanks for the Coronation stamps – Tom Stobart is delighted – and for many other things thanks.

Give my regards to H.T.C., to Janet who wrote from Auckland, Norm E. and many others. Love to Mum and Dad and the brothers and sisters.

More from India – if not then England.

Cheers, George.

Wengers Hotel, Delhi
26th June 1953

Dear Betty,

Rest and peace at last – the heat, a searing 112°F plus high humidity is a little discomodium but the private flat with fans and a very efficient personal valet in the U.K. High Commissioner's set of private flats is very, very pleasant.

Wow – another wallop of mail from England, Australia, Norway, America, N.Z. and S. Africa – what fun it is to have a fan mail. Already unknown women are writing – this is quite fun. Most are N.Z.ers who knew me and are now spread over the globe.

I should try and get down some of the happenings in Katmandu – I'll never recapture the whole tale, as it was more fantastic and fast moving than the ascent days.

On 20th June we reached Katmandu, but I must hop back to the morning of the 18th when we reached a place called Chaubas, the last camp with a view of the Himalaya and the cool breezes of 7,000 ft. It was a pleasant camp and everyone was beginning to feel the excitement of seeing the Embassy, of baths, silver salvers, wine with the meat course and long, lazy sofas.

On the 19th we were ready for away at 5 a.m., and pushed off for the long 4,500 ft drop to the Sun Kosi river and heat. As we left, I saw Tenzing surrounded by some Nepalis and in heated conversation. We greeted them and passed on. As we jolted down the track we passed a stream of people going up and they wanted to know where Tenzing and Hillary were. Ed and I were together and looked so skinny and puny that they didn't even think that Ed was who he was and passed on. Their main desire was to see Tenzing. We reached the Sun Kosi and there were a dozen newspaper men there with movie and still cameras and again they were mildly interested in us and sought Tenzing. T. came down and was surrounded, garlanded and covered with red powder (a doubtful honour being covered in this muck!).

We breakfasted and moved on in ghastly heat to a place called Hooksey. John Hunt and his wife met us there – they had walked out one day's march to meet us.

He warned us of the furore that the ascent had caused in India and Nepal, and told us of the frantic bitterness that the Press had built up over (1) the nationality of T. and (2) his superiority over Europeans and cited how he had reached the summit ahead of Ed and so made Ed "the second conqueror of Mt. Everest". All this was disappointing and rather disgusting after the great effort and the pleasure that we thought had been given.

John was disturbed, and went to see Tenzing and warn him of the controversies he would meet. He met T. and was told by the band of Nepalis who were with him that they had a signed statement from T. to say (1) I am a Nepali and (2) I reached the top 15 ft ahead of Hillary.

When T. heard this he was amazed but admitted that he had signed a paper, but complained that he could not read Nepali (in fact he cannot read or write – he can sign with his name in English and write his address).

We spent the night at Hooksey and several rival bands of political party types, a tribe of camera men and a flush of reporters spent the night at our camp. ('Life Magazine', 'Times', 'Daily Express', 'Daily Telegraph', 'Observer', 'Daily Mail', A.P.A., Reuters, plus three Indian papers, were all represented by their best correspondents).

Moving or talking was almost impossible without being photographed or overheard. Every newsman was ferreting for some 'new angle' and trying to keep it from the others. What a filthy system it all is – they slap each other on the back and drink together all the time double-crossing to scoop their companions.

The morning following, we were shocked to hear the Indian radio brag about the statement that had been obtained from T. to say that he had reached the top ahead of Ed – the radio went on to say how he had guided and pulled the party up Everest. The team effort was forgotten and the fact that Ed and T. as a 'rope' were a climbing unit was carefully squashed. Old John went hopping mad but after consultation realised the political implications and regretfully decided to avoid a row – which, it seems, is exactly what was wanted. And so to cut a tedious story short, we approached Katmandu feeling disillusioned about the sacrifices made to put T. on top, about politics, newspapers and all plainsmen in general.

On 20th we set out at 5 a.m. and after five hours walking reached Banepa where jeeps and cars had managed the rough route. Thousands were there to meet us. Three distinct Nepali political parties were competing with each other crying "Tenzing Zindabar", "Tenzing Nepali Ho!" "The first man to conquer Mt. Everest" (this by one man with a loud speaker and followed by the party marching and crying in rhythm) "Tenzing Sherpa".

The noise, the amplifiers, the crowds, the cheer leaders and excitement was most moving – moving me and the other boys to disgust and the Nepalis to a frenzy of hero worship. T. arrived and was swept onto a prepared stage, garlanded and cheered. John and Ed were at first left out then someone decided to push them up. All in all, it was a riotous shambles, where John and Ed were treated most rudely. Luckily we were quite ignored, popped into some friendly jeeps and pushed off for Katmandu.

A triumphal procession had been arranged – for Tenzing – and they drove to the outskirts of Katmandu, the route lined with people. A dozen triumphal arches had been built with pictures of T. on Everest holding the Nepal flag, T. on top pulling up Ed, who was on his knees, and so on. At the edge of the city we passed the royal carriage with four horses – all decorated over lavishly with flowers and finery. I nearly hurt myself laughing when I thought of Ed and John in a carriage and four driving to the palace in this. The mixture of ceremony and ludicrous farce caused us no end

On the team's return to Kathmandu thousands of people came out to meet Tenzing. Triumphal arches declared his victory and the frenzied crowds roared in celebration.

of mirth. If the whole show had been filmed you would think on seeing it, to be an overdrawn mixture of Chaplin, Laurel and Hardy with the Marx Brothers thrown in.

Finally, the 'honoured' three arrived and clambered aboard the four-man carriage, along with the chairman of the reception committee – then Mrs. Tenzing and her two daughters – and two postillions, and two women leaders of the reception committee, and one other unidentified body. Twelve in all in the four-man royal coach!

Tenzing set on a vegetable crate high in the centre. Ed and John were polite and waited for the ladies to be seated and finished by having standing room and they promptly sat on the floor with just their heads poking over the coach sides. Nepali hats were popped on their heads, a couple of garlands round their necks and dusted with a red powder in their hair and faces (a mark of honour).

The crowds surged and roared and squashed in unchecked, the horses plunged and fought with postillions, and with a jerk that toppled everyone in the carriage, they set off. I shall never forget the mirth it caused us. John and Ed were by this time browned off and smarting under the indelicacy with which they were being received. It was true, but we laughed on. Their treatment was highly insulting, while more seriously still T. was not being treated as a returning Hero – but a God. The national feeling that the climb by T. had aroused was the strongest ever raised in Nepal and in the next three days it manifest itself in many ways, particularly in a hatred of India.

This was the first political demonstration I had ever seen and there I saw the Communist party with wild mad cheer leaders growing hoarse, backed by hundreds of school kids who chanted the slogans. It was quite a disturbing sight to see how effective they were.

Thus began the triumphal procession which lasted two hours and pulled up at the town hall. There Ed, John and T. appeared on the balcony and speeches were made. Then Ed and John who had seen us waved from the balcony and carelessly wandered to the parapet, sat on it with legs dangling over the crowd, tired, thirsty, dirty, but now the humour of it caught them and forgetting respect and decorum, they burlesqued without disguise.

From the Town Hall the procession went to the King's Palace. All this time we followed in a jeep – Greg and Tom sat on the bonnet while I sat on the roof, bearded, dirty, in a torn shirt and tennis shoes. I had a great view of everything, and because of my conspicuous position and Ed's inconspicuous one in the well of the coach, I received (and acknowledged) many cheers on his behalf. Whenever Ed and John caught sight of us, we waved and laughed, and their faces lost their gloomy looks and they enjoyed the joke on their ignominious situation.

We reached the Palace at 7 p.m. – Ed and John had been continuously in a procession and in the coach for 7½ hours without drink, food, or a chance to relieve themselves and they were tired. Ed had a cold which took his voice clean away, they were covered in brownish red powder, and with Nepali hats they looked just like a couple of Cairo wags.

At the Palace, a company of Gurkas sloped arms, the band played anthems, horns tooted, while scarlet-coated footmen rushed around. We all went up the marble stairs and into the huge, gaudy, chandeliered hall and sat with the dignitaries (a misnomer!!) of Nepal. The P.M. received us – the Queens (1st and 2nd) and the King. The ceremony was short and to the point.

First T. was given the title "Star of the Twilight" and a sash with a large star similar to the Garter star. He is entitled to call himself Tara Tenzing (the equivalent of highest knighthood – a rare honour in this country, usually bestowed on royalty, Ranas, and Maharajahs only). Then Ed received a citation in English and Nepali, plus a crimson sash and a maroon and silver star and the title of "Gurka Right Hand – First Class" (there are four classes). John got the same.

But the form and the dress we were in was most amusing. Ed was in ski trousers and wind jacket, John in shorts, tennis shoes and army command jacket, most of us in tennis shoes with torn shirts and all with beards. Griff Pugh was most ludicrous in a pair of stripped pyjamas and four months of red hair over his ears. That, I'm sure, will be the only royal investiture in such disreputable rig.

After that we were more or less free. John and Ed reached the Embassy more exhausted than they had been on Everest. We had a wonderful dinner at the Embassy and fell into bed about midnight.

The next four days were tough for Ed and John, with political navigation in treacherous waters – mixed with receptions, tea parties, press conferences, where the Press tried to "get the truth" – in other words get a difference in stories between Ed and T. and then make capital of it. Tenzing was offered 2 lakhs of rupees (200,000 rupees) to say he reached the top first. He refused to and appealed to John (this was his first chance to talk to John without being 'shepherded' by his Nepali friends who were brow-beating and trying to force his hand) – and between John and Koirala, the P.M., they gave him a permanent police escort.

I escaped the daily official affairs and spent three days with Wilf Noyce in packing and making an inventory of the equipment being shipped to England (tents, primuses, oxygen sets for demonstration, 50 oxygen bottles R.A.F. being returned, wirelesses, tools, pressure cookers, crampons, ice axes, and so on).

The first evening was taken up with a reception and cocktail party at the British Embassy followed by a banquet dinner. The next with a similar reception at the Indian Embassy followed by a buffet dinner with the officers of the Indian Military mission – we had a band playing dinner music and all – just like the films. I forget where the last night was – oh yes – we had a barbecue with the American colony – 11 families living communally and working on agricultural education and aid – called Point Four Plan.

Two days ago John, Ed, Tenzing and Greg flew to Calcutta for two days of formality and today they are due in for four more here.

Two days ago, we (Pugh, Stobart, Noyce, Band, Westmacott and self) flew to Patna from Katmandu. Stayed a night there – where I met a Mary O'Connell from Dunedin (Med. School lecturer) who is doing U.N.E.S.C.O. work in T.B. Stayed the night with her and flew here yesterday, stopping en route at Benares and Lucknow. (5 hour flight in Dakota – the Indian inland airways are very slap-happy, badly timed and careless.) A dust storm over Delhi held us up for 2 hours and we came in on a very shaky landing.

And now the political aspects of this are dying down. The various stories of who was first? what nationality is T.? did we say T. was a poor climber? – and a dozen other bits of nastiness have almost gone from the Indian press. It seems a fact that the Indian Press in general are very anti-British and their vituperative

News of the Everest triumph soon spread around the world and images of expedition members were used across all sorts of advertising.

abilities are most ably developed. The virtuosity they show in twisting a story is far greater than any British paper!

There is another chapter that should be written to this tale. I've given snatches of it before, because it began with Izzard at the beginning – The Press and Everest.

The Press have sent their most experienced newsmen in to try and break the copyright of the 'The Times'. They were prepared to pay anything to get to the big news – "Everest climbed" – first. 'The Daily Telegraph' had Colin Reid (a whisky soak and the nastiest piece of goods in the game) who spent £15,000 plus! (the cost of our whole expedition) in bribing and working for the news. He was paying £87 a week to have the telephones and telegraph system monitored and he covered the wireless waves too. He offered £5,000 to Fletcher, the Embassy wireless operator for the news.

The Indian telegraph office here is rotten with graft and the correspondence haunted the office to milk the news from James Morris (the Times correspondent with us) despatches. All the newsmen here – quoting Morris, Hutchinson (Times), Matua (Telegraph), Smith (Daily Express), Jackson (Reuters) – all say "this is the worst, most cut-throat, double crossing newspaper war they have ever known", and that it seems is saying something.

The arguments as to whether the 'Times' has a right to world news and a copyright on the story is hotly debated. The Ambassador was attacked by the news-hawks to say he was aiding and abetting by sending the message in code through Foreign Office channels, questions were asked in 'The House' and so on. It's a long, long tale of intrigue, squabble and bribery – a sordid, dirty chapter of the Everest story.

Of them all, Izzard has come out the best. He was rudely received by us, but we feel he has played fairly. He worked and walked for his stories and what I have seen they are quite good stuff. He saw early on that the 'Times' man was too active and able to beat on the icefall (James Morris, with our aid reached Camp IV and went up and down the icefall three times – he was at IV when we came down with the news) and he returned to Katmandu and saw the correspondents here fabricating reports from rumour, saw the bribery and went home disgusted. Our respect for him has risen greatly.

I'm sweating quietly and tired of writing. I have a lot of 'thank-you' notes to write so I had better stop.

The first batch of my cyclostyled letters arrived from Keki yesterday. I was worried about this letter, because Keki is not beyond opening this – and so far he has shown no respect for the trust of mountain news given. A long article under his name appeared – with photographs – in the Indian papers on Ed and his achievements, facts taken from our letters to him. Last year he informed the newspapers of what we wrote him from Cho Oyu and this year we shut up. He used several of my Garwhal photographs and so on. I'm afraid if he gets copies of these Everest letters he will use them. Be most careful about what you send through him. This is not meant to be unfriendly – but he is too enthusiastic, he can't hold any news to himself and he seems to see no wrong in making capital of it. We have written frankly to him, complaining of his actions, but he sees no reason for our complaint and thinks he is doing us a favour by advertising our achievements. If you have sent any more through him, write him a letter and ask him to air-mail it straight to me.

The shirts arrived, the morning I left Katmandu. Many thanks. Best wishes to all. In less than a week we'll all be in London (2nd July) and the next few days here in Delhi will certainly be most interesting. We are really having quite a prolonged 'Cinderella at the Ball' experience – with lots of Alice in Wonderland thrown in. I wonder where it will all end?

Smiles and pleasant hours to all,

George.

* * *

AFTERWORD

Peter Hillary

George's personality shines through from the flanks of Mount Everest in these letters to his sister Betty and his family and friends. His humour and his ability to see things positively are woven into his missives from the front line – he is a terrific writer just as he was a wonderful raconteur.

George was given the great responsibility of pushing the route up the Lhotse Face, which was the critical upper-mountain barrier to making summit attempts. The hard ice and the grinding effects of the altitude wore them down but after two weeks of team effort they reached the South Col and the climb was 'on'. George inveigled his way into more of John Hunt's plans for more high altitude sorties on Everest and he was the only man left on the Col at 26,000 ft when Ed Hillary and Tenzing Norgay struck out for the top. It was to George that my father revealed their success in the rough-and-ready language between close friends.

After the Everest endeavour many hoped that Himalayan climbing could settle down into a more normal routine, but of course the summit was just the beginning. Attaining the highest

THE WEEKLY NEWS

With which is Incorporated "THE WEEKLY GRAPHIC AND NEW ZEALAND MAIL"

AUCKLAND, WEDNESDAY, SEPTEMBER 9, 1953

NEW ZEALAND'S WEDDING OF THE YEAR: SIR EDMUND HILLARY AND HIS CHARMING BRIDE

The conqueror of Everest, Sir Edmund Hillary, and Lady Hillary (formerly Miss Louise Rose) smile happily as they leave the chapel of the Diocesan High School, Auckland, through an archway of ice-axes after their wedding last Thursday. They are attended by Miss Rosalie Goodyear, of Atherton, as bridesmaid, and Mr George Lowe, Sir Edmund's close friend and climbing companion, as best man. A "quiet" wedding had been planned, but 1500 people thronged the streets to acclaim the couple and to wish them well.

On 3 September 1953, Ed married Louise Rose in Auckland and friends from the New Zealand Alpine Club formed an archway of ice-axes. Behind Ed is clean-shaven George Lowe, his best man that day.

point on earth came to symbolise an ultimate achievement against great odds and that symbolism of humankind pushing the boundaries has stuck. Throughout my upbringing, wherever we went in the world I would hear, 'That's Ed Hillary. That's him. He was the first man to climb Everest'. While my father was 6 foot 2 inches tall most people thought he was a foot taller than that; you could see it in their eyes, that excitement – wonderment even – of meeting someone who had gone into the unknown.

Climbing the world's highest mountain in 1953 was an astounding achievement. Mount Everest is on the cusp of the physiological limits of what people can climb and throwing in the brutal weather, the difficulty of the final ascent, the debilitating effects of the altitude and the long duration of the expedition it is impressive that they not only climbed the mountain but did not lose a single man. Perhaps most importantly they saw their achievement as a team effort – they all played a part in putting two men on the top. Today, with our improved knowledge of the mountain and of climbing at altitude we continue to lose lives in the icefall and up in the 'death zone' and today's climbers largely consider their own success the only objective. But that is not how George Lowe played the game as one of the members of the 1953 British Mount Everest Expedition.

Some people talk about today's climbers on Everest in dismissive tones but I don't agree that the mountain should be off limits to those who want to test themselves upon it. Most of them, myself included, are largely up there for the crazy thrill of it all, riddled with ego and ambition, fear and even uncomprehending – 'what the … am I doing here' – when faced with repeated opportunities to depart this mortal coil. Whatever might be said of the modern face of climbing on Everest, it is still a demanding and exacting prospect whichever way you look at it. For the really great mountaineers among us there are three mountain walls and two rearing ridgelines that rarely see a human set foot on them. The opportunities for adventure on Everest are still wide open.

And that is what is so magical about George's letters. They exude the excitement of a man on a grand adventure where the outcome is uncertain and the spoils are beyond belief – to stand on top of the world. As the great French mountaineer Lionel Terray put it, we are 'Conquistadors of the Useless', perhaps, but the benefits are a lifetime of satisfaction that you made a supreme effort in the face of your own fears. For me to have *been there*, whether it is high in the Hornbein Couloir on the American West Ridge route without ropes or on the South Summit of the South-East Ridge at dawn, *being there* is something you cannot take away from those who decide to put everything on the line.

That is what drew me to go to Everest and that is why I am glad I did. And that is why George Lowe was a serial adventurer too. George, thank you for your achievement on the big 'E' and for your love of life. While most of us dabble with our dreams, you just did it. You are the real thing!

* * *

Back home in New Zealand, Ed and George were given a heroes' welcome. A local newspaper carried this cartoon of the pair, with the title 'NEVEREST!'

In 1954 the pair waved goodbye to New Zealand once more, heading back to the Himalayas to explore the regions east of Everest.

THOUGHTS

Here's the top peak; the multitude below
Live, for they can, there:
This man decided not to Live but Know –
Bury this man there?
Here – here's his place, where meteors shoot, clouds form,
Lightnings are loosened,
Stars come and go ...

> Robert Browning, 1855

What is the use of climbing Mount Everest? If you cannot understand that there is something in man which responds to the challenge of this mountain and goes out to meet it, that the struggle is the struggle of life itself upward and forever upward, then you won't see why we go. What we get from this adventure is just sheer joy. And joy is, after all, the end of life.

> George Mallory, 1922

But we feel it is a great moment in our lives – in fact one of the best we have ever experienced. We think that something is going to happen; we hope devoutly that something will happen; yet at the same time we do not want to be hurt or killed. What is it then that we do want? It is that lure of youth – adventure, and adventure for adventure's sake.

> Winston Churchill, 1930

Useless toil, why endure it? Then I thought, with an inward grin, what a fuss there would be if we reached the summit. We would have to endure long adulatory speeches, our digestions would be ruined by innumerable dinners, we would be pestered by autograph hunters. Here on Everest, at least, there was peace.

Frank Smythe, 1937

In these days of upheaval and violent change, when the basic values of today are the vain and shattered dreams of tomorrow, there is much to be said for a philosophy which aims at living a full life while the opportunity offers. There are few treasures of more lasting worth than the experience of a way of life that is in itself wholly satisfying. Such, after all, are the only possessions of which no fate, no cosmic catastrophe can deprive us; nothing can alter the fact if for one moment in eternity we have really lived.

Eric Shipton, 1943

Was it all worthwhile? For us who took part in the venture, it was so beyond doubt. We have shared a high endeavour; we have witnessed scenes of beauty and grandeur; we have built up a lasting comradeship among ourselves and we have seen the fruits of that comradeship ripen into achievement. We shall not forget those moments of great living upon that mountain.

John Hunt, 1953

Everest stands firm. Its flanks and ridges are often cluttered with climbers and it may ever be this way. Perhaps we are somehow to blame for this – we opened the door, we showed the way. We made men and women believe the impossible. We experienced the elation that comes through overcoming anxieties and then mastering our fears in some genuinely tough and life-threatening situations. But we chose to be there and that is the thing. We all chose to take a risk when others, just as able, might have turned back. We rode our luck and we were blessed in return. Our achievement, I hope, will last as long as there are adventurous hearts out there; as long as people still raise their eyes to the summits, and take on a challenge in the simple way that we did – slow and sure, head up, just one step at a time.

George Lowe, 2013

FURTHER READING

John Hunt, *The Ascent of Everest* (London: Hodder & Stoughton, 1953). Alfred Gregory, *The Picture of Everest* (London: Hodder & Stoughton, 1954). Wilfrid Noyce, *South Col* (London: William Heinemann, 1954). Edmund Hillary, *High Adventure* (London: Hodder & Stoughton, 1955). Edmund Hillary and George Lowe, *East of Everest* (London: Hodder & Stoughton, 1956). Jan Morris, *Coronation Everest* (London: Faber & Faber, 1958). George Lowe, *Because it is There* (London: Cassell, 1959). Tom Hornbein, *Everest: The West Ridge* (London: Allen & Unwin, 1966). Chris Bonington, *Everest: The Hard Way* (London: Hodder & Stoughton, 1976).George Band, *Everest: Fifty Years on Top of the World* (London: Collins, 2003). Michael Ward, *Everest: A Thousand Years of Exploration* (London: Ernest Press, 2003). George Lowe and Huw Lewis-Jones, *The Conquest of Everest: Original Photographs from the Legendary First Ascent* (London: Thames & Hudson, 2013).

BIOGRAPHIES

GEORGE LOWE is a New Zealand-born explorer, mountaineer, photographer and filmmaker. He was a leading high-altitude climber on the 1953 British Everest Expedition, on which his best friend Edmund Hillary and Sherpa Tenzing Norgay became the first men to summit the world's highest peak. As well as taking photographs throughout this journey, Lowe directed the Oscar-nominated documentary *The Conquest of Everest* and the following year again joined Hillary to climb in the Himalaya. He was official photographer of the Commonwealth Trans-Antarctic Expedition, which, between 1955 and 1958, not only traversed Antarctica but also became the first to reach the South Pole overland since Captain Scott in 1912. In later years a teacher, Lowe was the founder and first Chairman of the Himalayan Trust in Britain.

DR HUW LEWIS-JONES is a historian of exploration with a PhD from the University of Cambridge. Huw was Curator at the Scott Polar Research Institute and the National Maritime Museum and is now an award-winning author who writes and lectures widely about adventure and the visual arts. His books include *Arctic*, *Ocean Portraits*, *In Search of the South Pole*, and *Mountain Heroes*, which won Adventure Book of the Year at the World ITB Awards in Germany. His latest book is *The Conquest of Everest*, co-written with George Lowe.

JAN MORRIS is a celebrated British travel writer and historian. Jan's first experience of mountaineering was her assignment to cover the 1953 Everest expedition for *The Times* but she now lives with her partner Elizabeth among the mountains at the top left-hand corner of Wales, and there she has written some fifty books of travel, history, memoir and imagination. She is an Honorary DLitt of the University of Wales, a member of the Gordedd of Bards and an Honorary Student of her old Oxford college, Christ Church. She has four children, eight grandchildren and a Norwegian Forest Cat, named Ibsen.

PETER HILLARY first climbed Mount Everest in 1990, and repeated this feat again in 2002 on a *National Geographic*-sponsored ascent. With such a famous father as Sir Edmund, it was perhaps inevitable that Peter's life would be drawn to the mountains. He has now completed more than forty expeditions and, like his father, is deeply involved in development projects for the Sherpa people in the Everest region of Nepal. George Lowe is Peter's godfather.

Right: George and Ed gathered together a small team in the New Zealand Alps over Christmas in 1950, and on the reverse of this photograph is scribbled a typical conversation they'd have before a big climb. The best way, they soon discovered, was just to have a go! This kind of optimism is the heartbeat of adventure and their skill and enthusiasm for the mountains would soon take them to the Himalayas and later Everest, the greatest challenge of them all.